Images of Hawaii

Text copyright ©1984 by Leonard Lueras.
Photographs copyright ©1984 by the individual photographers who are credited on the book's inside back cover. All rights reserved.
This book, or parts thereof, may not be reproduced in any form without permission in writing from Hong Kong Publishing Company, Ltd., 307, Yu Yuet Lai Building, 43-55 Wyndham Street, Central, Hong Kong.
Published by Hong Kong Publishing Company, Ltd.
Series Design by Werner Hahn.

Printed in Hong Kong by New Champion Printing Company Limited.
Colour separation by Universal Colour Scanning Ltd. Hong Kong.

Art Directed by The Wanderer, Inc., Honolulu.
Typography by Innovative Media, Inc., Honolulu.
ISBN: 962-7035-15-7

Images of Hawaii

Written and Produced by Leonard Lueras

With Photographic Contributions by
Warren Bolster, Joe Carini, Tom Chapman, Daphne Chu,
Nicki Clancey, Dana Edmunds, Peter French,
Lew Harrington, Jeff Helberg, Ron Jett, Val Kim,
Leonard Lueras, Meleanna Pricher, Frank Salmoiraghi,
Steve Shrader, Greg Vaughn and William Waterfall

The expressive Hawaiians, a proud Polynesian people with a rich and poetical linguistic tradition, have numerous words in their vocabulary to describe differing concepts—and intensities—of light. In ancient chants *(mele)* they sing of dazzling light *(hulili)*, torchlight *(aulama)*, basic daylight *('eleao)* and even sacred light *(la'akea)*. And in more recent, technological times they have added quaint expressions such as *kukui uila*, which romantically analyzes electric light as being a luminous combination of glowing *kukui* candlenuts and lightning, and *kukui pa'a lima* ("light held in one's hand"), which identifies a flashlight.

All the above are charming appellations, but perhaps the most beautiful and radiant Hawaiian word of all is *melemele*, a lyrical and mellifluous Hawaiian word that refers to the golden, honey-colored light of early morning and late afternoon. Photographers well know this light as that special splash of warm orange-amber that illuminates what they call "the magic hour." It's a perfect, yellowish light that makes Kodachrome film scream, weakens a picture editor's will to resist, and inspires *maitai*-drinking authors to poesy.

Indeed, from quiet Naalehu town at the southernmost tip of the Hawaiian Islands chain to tiny Kure Atoll some 1,367 miles away in the archipelago's northwest corner, this light frames, punctuates and sets aglow many of the "images" reproduced in this book. It has also, for more than two centuries, strongly fixed "return again" visions of Hawaii on the emulsion of every Hawaii visitor's mind.

Melemele. For many years before photographers first visited Hawaii (beginning with traveling daguerrotypists in 1845), most painterly visions of this tropical place concentrated on this light. In Vermeer and Weyeth-like oils, or in more muted watercolor washes, visiting artists tried over and over to capture the campy but timeless grandeur of a Waikiki, Lahaina or Niihau sunset, or the soft morning mauves and peaches that transform the Islands' crenellated *palis* (cliffs) and *pu'u* (volcanic cinder cones) into massive crowns and tiaras. These painters regularly created and distributed such visions of Paradise with great success, despite what media critics called—and still call—a cliché "South Seas" treatment. Cliché? Maybe, but such artists, and later photographers, were and still are on to something. They knew then, and still know, that soothing sunrises and sunsets sell.

According to a recent commercial media survey conducted in Honolulu, the best-selling postcard im-

Facing page: Late afternoon *melemele* sunlight lingers at twilight and on the Dillingham Transportation Building in downtown Honolulu's Bishop Street "business district."
Above: Honolulu Harbor's Aloha Tower, Hawaii's "first highrise building," welcomes visiting ships beneath the charms of late afternoon mist and a fine Honolulu rainbow.

Above: A crew of *repoussé* canoeists recall ancient Hawaiian voyaging days.
On facing page: Modern-day outrigger paddlers glide past a sparkling skyline on the *mauka* side of Waikiki.

ages of Hawaii are *by far* those that feature a basic sunset (or sunrise) that bathes offshore waters with what surf photographers call "the sparkle factor." Even better, say the owners of Waikiki souvenir shops, is a photograph that includes not *just* a sunset or sunrise, but, for extra measure, a saucy Hawaiian rainbow. Under such *melemele* circumstances, rainbows or not, even mundane objects — such as harbor-side storage tanks or abandoned cars in a *kiawe* thicket — come to special life and gleam like a realist's "found objects." Harsh shadows disappear and what was once squinty glare stops down into a distinct color spectrum.

Ansel Adams, the late and grand old man of American photography, wrote in 1964 that "no place on earth is more exciting [than Hawaii] to both the serious photographer and the snapshooter." He said that "certain bold features, such as the Napali Coast, the jagged splendor of the *pali* and the cliffs and the cinder cones of Haleakala [Crater] are as dramatic and awe-inspiring as any scenic displays of their kind in the world." Adams acknowledged, however, that Hawaii's "soft landscapes, colors accented by bright flowers, costumes and sunsets" are "more favorable to color photographs" than to Adams-style black and white photography.

Those of us who live here — and photograph here — agree. But what we find really impressive and magical

This heroic bronze panel appears at the base of the golden Kamehameha the Great statue in front of Honolulu's Judiciary Building. It tells the story of how Kamehameha singlehandedly warded off the spears of attacking warriors during a Big Island power struggle

about this fine local light are those quiet and eerie moments when the sun's rays arch across the Pacific and illuminate those special people, places and things we consider to be uniquely Hawaiian. This optical segregation begins with the *aina,* the land, and *kai,* the sea, then radiates outward to the *keiki aina,* the children of the land, and finally focuses on the faces and cultural traditions of the fast-disappearing Hawaiians.

Truly classical reminders of the ancient Hawaiians and their culture are tough to find these days (outside of museums and private collections), but they are here, and they have somehow endured and survived some 200 years of accelerated "culture shock" and "modernization." The most obvious and impressive of these relics are the many lava rock *heiau,* or temples, that you will find rising from jungle tangles or squatting like lonely, primeval beacons on prominent headlands. These *heiau* are serious, archaeological relics, but just as important, and somehow more charming, are the hundreds of seemingly animated petroglyphs, or "pictures in stone," that the Hawaiians left here and there on large stones or in lava fields to document the little and big things that their "Stone Age" society took seriously. These whimsical glyphs are the oldest, purely "pictorial" records we have of old Hawaii. They are primitive by oriental and occidental graphical stan-

Above left: This *bas relief* in white marble sits outside the Mission Houses Museum in Honolulu and commemorates the first printing press in the Hawaiian Islands. Frockcoated missionaries watch as a caped and helmeted Hawaiian apprentice mans the press.
Above right: Details of Hawaiian documents held in the hand of a statue of Hawaii's last queen, Liliuokalani, who was overthrown by American businessmen in 1893. This work, located between Iolani Palace and the State Capitol Mall, was sculpted by the artist Marianna Pineda.
Below left: British-style escutcheons decorate the Kalakaua coronation stand that sits on the Iolani Palace's old royal parkgrounds.

Above: Members of the Hawaiian Royal Guard honor the memory of Hawaii's last queen, Liliuokalani, in formal ceremonies held recently at Iolani Palace.
At left: Royal Guard attendants display a silver ceremonial vessel once owned by Hawaii's last and very popular king, David Kalakaua.

Above: Kalakaua descendants gather in the Kalakaua family tomb at the Royal Mausoleum in Nuuanu to pray and sing tributes to the late King on the occasion of his birthday.

dards, but they speak volumes about a place that wasn't formally "discovered" by Westerners until the British navigator Captain James Cook called here in 1778.

Not unlike the contemporary "images" shot and then printed in this book, these petroglyphs communicate much older (but still applicable and educational) truths about such diverse things as ancient fishing techniques, celestial movements, genealogical origins, surfboard riding, specific positions and movements in classical *hula*-dancing and even sexuality and the birthing process. At certain latter-day petroglyph sites you'll even find Hawaiians making bemused "contact" with the *haole,* or outsider. On one stone will be a stick man who is awkwardly trying to ride one of Hawaii's first imported horses, and on yet another he'll be seen firing an unwieldy musket . . . or paddling his canoe up to a visiting schooner . . . or wearing a strange European hat.

With today's highly-evolved cameras, we are able to capture and shape more sophisticated and recognizable "images" of Hawaii, but the message, however sharp or realistic, remains the same: People change, socially, physically and even culturally, and their means of expression differ from century to century or year to year, but they still live under a common sun that lights common truths. This particular kind of "light" is what the Hawaiian people of old called *malamalama,* or "the

Facing page: The Big Island's celebrated Kanakaole sisters, Nalani and Pualani, prepare for a classical hula performance at the Volcano. Left and above: Nalani and Pualani begin chanting in earnest, and a member of their Hula Halau 'o Kekuhi breaks into spirited dance.

light of knowledge." It is an abstract term that implies a clear and shining train of thought.

With such light in mind, take another look at the sunlit Hawaiian coat-of-arms that appears opposite this book's title page. At the base of that European-esque logo, beneath a pair of *kahili* standard bearers wearing royal Hawaiian feather cloaks, you will see an inscription that proclaims in Hawaiian *Ua Mau Ke Ea O Ka Aina I Ka Pono*. That slogan, which today is the State of Hawaii's official motto, was uttered by the Hawaiian King Kamehameha III on July 31, 1843, shortly after his kingdom was given back to him and his people by Britain six months after an impulsive and misguided British sea captain had taken the Islands by force in the name of Queen Victoria and Great Britain.

During a moving Restoration Day ceremony held that day in central Honolulu, an apologetic British Rear-Admiral officially "gave" Hawaii back to the Hawaiians and the Kamehamehas. Kamehameha III quietly accepted this restoration of Hawaiian sovereignty, then turned to his people and, with tears in his eyes, assured them that whatever had happened to them — or would happen to them in the future — "The Life Of The Land Is Perpetuated in Righteousness."

With that wisdom as our *malamalama*, our guiding light, let's continue our travels through *Hawaii nei*.

No alien land in all the world has any deep strong charm for me, but that one; no other land could so longingly and so beseechingly haunt me, sleeping and waking, through half a lifetime, as that one has done. Other things leave me, but it abides; other things change, but it remains the same. For me its balmy airs are always blowing, its summer seas flashing in the sun; the pulsing of the surfbeat in my ear; I can see its garlanded crags, its leaping cascades, its plumy palms drowsing by the shore, its remote summits floating above the cloud rack; I can feel the spirit of its woodland solitudes, I can hear the plash of its brooks; in my nostrils still lives the breath of flowers that perished twenty years ago...

— Mark Twain, reminiscing in 1889 about his first and only visit to Hawaii.

On preceding pages: An *ohia* forest bursts into flame as a 1977 Pu'u Kia'i lava flow on the Big Island advances toward the sea and threatens Kalapana town. Facing page: A brave, visiting journalist walks toward a towering fountain generated by Vent 51 during the April, 1983 eruption of Pu'u Kahauale'a volcano. Above: Pu'u Kahauale'a dances the night away.

Yes, Paradise-lovers, even Mark Twain, that grand American master of understatement, social satire and biting wit, was obligingly seduced by Hawaii. But why not? Where else in the world can latter-day Huck Finns spend their mornings frolicking on a snow-covered slope, their afternoons riding horses through Texas-style rangelands, and then—before settling in for early-evening drinks and a look at a major volcanic eruption—go for a swim in the champagne-like waters of a surfblasted tidepool?

When it comes to nature, whether spectacular or sublime, this is *the* place on earth where you can experience Her to the max. International geologists, oceanographers and astronomers have long touted Hawaii as one of the world's finest and cleanest scientific observation sites. That's because the skies above her mountain tops are intensely clear and well-suited for celestial observation, her deep seas are rich in minerals and rare sea life and—for extra measure—her volcanoes explode regularly with new information about the origins of life.

Botanists are another matter altogether. Many of these most exacting of nature-lovers come here to spend a few pleasant days in the Hawaiian bush, then linger for weeks or even months as they try to untangle the mystery of Hawaii's more than 2,700 species, subspecies and other unique varieties of endemic flowering plants. As one eminent biologist wrote recently, "98 per cent of all Hawaiian flowering plants grow only in Hawaii and no place else on earth!"

During the last century, as reports of Hawaii's botanical wonders began reaching botanic societies throughout the world, these findings caused quite a stir in scientific circles. Even Charles Darwin (1809-1882),

the great British naturist who wrote the *Origin of Species,* once lamented in a letter that Hawaii was the one place in the world he had always wanted to study, but was never fortunate enough to visit. He knew, after having studied colleagues' Hawaiian field notes, that this was a special place indeed.

In their oral traditions, ancient Polynesians called this pristine landfall north of the South Seas *Hawai'ia,* or "Burning Hawaii," in deference to her active, exploding volcanoes. Then, as now, this was the newest place on earth, a primeval, tropical chain of emerald isles aglow with fire and life. And today, more than a dozen centuries after a first crew of Marquesan voyagers sailed north and landed on her southernmost shores, those same fires still burn and glow much as they did at the time of The Creation.

If you are ever fortunate enough to be here when the southern Big Island of Hawaii begins vibrating with nervous twitches that geologists call "harmonic tremor," hop onto an interisland aircraft and hope to be on the Big Island when the volcano goddess Pele rushes to the surface and explodes in one of her mad dances of fire and fury. You will soon understand just how insignificant and ephemeral our concepts of time, power and nature really are. The spectre of a Hawaiian volcano roaring and spouting above a vast lava moonscape

In late 1984, Mauna Loa, the largest active volcano in the world, erupted for the first time in a decade and generated a red-hot show that dazzled the world's press and geologists. In this spectacular photo a Honolulu-based camera crew hikes toward one of her brilliant "curtains of fire."

will be the most humbling experience of your life. It's the Apocalypse found.

This still visible Hawaiian creation process began some 60 million years ago during a prehistoric period scientists refer to as the mid-Tertiary Era. At that time huge masses of molten lava broke through the floor of the Hawaiian Deep and began rising, inch by inch, through some 16,000 feet of seawater to the Pacific Ocean's surface. Because the center of this underwater volcanic activity kept moving to the south (in a W.N.W. to E.S.E. crescent of fire across the Tropic of Cancer), it eventually fashioned a neat archipelago that now runs for nearly 1,600 miles (between 154° 40' and 178° 75' W longitude, and 18° 54' to 28° 15' N latitude). What you see today, in effect, is a series of some 132 mountain peaks that have risen from the sea, broken the ocean's surface, and accommodated life, each in their own peculiar way.

The oldest and still generally uninhabited of these islands—the so-called Northwestern Hawaiian Islands, or "Leeward Islands"—are an odd collection of shoals, atolls and islets that cater only to passing ships, thousands of common and rare sea birds and the occasional Coast Guard or naval signal station. Midway Island, which gained notoriety as a World War II staging area, might be familiar to some people, but most of

these islands—with exotic names such as Kure, Lisianski, French Frigate Shoals and Hermes—are relatively unknown, even though they are legally part of the City and County of Honolulu.

Down south, however, are the more familiar "major islands" of Hawaii—Oahu, Kauai, Molokai, Lanai, Maui, Hawaii, Niihau and Kahoolawe—and it is here that all significant human life, contemporary cultural activity and the outside world's vision of Hawaii is concentrated. These are those same mid-Pacific landfalls that our man Twain called "the loveliest fleet of islands anchored in any sea."

They are the newest of the many Hawaiian Islands, but for some unknown reason they have evolved into the lushest and biggest land masses in the fleet. Rising above the spacious Big Island, for example, are two massive volcanic peaks—Mauna Kea ("White Mountain") and Mauna Loa ("Long Mountain")—often identified by geologists as this planet's highest mountain peaks. These shield volcanoes only protrude 13,796 and 13,677 feet respectively above sea level, but scientists like to point out that from their bases at the bottom of the ocean to their sometimes snow-covered summits, these mountains have risen to a vertical height of some 30,000 feet, or even higher than Mt. Everest in the central Asian Himalayas.

During the winter, snow-capped Mauna Kea provides a decidedly non-Hawaiian looking backdrop for Big Island cattle quietly grazing in sub-tropical pastures.

The first Westerner to comment on these striking monoliths was, coincidentally, the only American who traveled with Captain Cook during his final 1776-1779 voyage to the Pacific in search of a Northwest Passage. That Connecticut Yankee in Captain Cook's crew was a young adventurer, John Ledyard, who, contrary to orders from the British Admiralty, wrote and published a book about his Hawaii adventures that beat Cook, his officers and the Admiralty into print by a full year.

Shortly after sailing into the Sandwich Islands (as Cook had named Hawaii, after his voyage's sponsor, John Montagu, the fourth Earl of Sandwich and the First Lord of the British Admiralty), Ledyard wrote in his log that he was struck by the sheer mass of Hawaii's mountains, which during a February, 1779 visit were "sharp" and "caped with snow."

"Owyhee has every appearance in nature," he wrote, "to suppose it once to have been a volcano. Its height, magnitude, shape and perhaps its situation indicate not only that, but that its original formation was effected by such a cause. The eastern side of the island is one continued bed of lava from the summit to the sea, and under the sea in 50 fathoms water some distance from the shore; and this side of the Island [is] utterly barren and devoid of even a single shrub. But there is no tradition among the inhabitants of any such circumstances."

No tradition? Ledyard was wrong, of course, because the Hawaiians' mythology is rich in stories about periodic volcanic activity, but perhaps he had just talked to the wrong native guides. If he had met the right *kahuna* (teacher), he would have heard about Pele, the great volcano goddess who was born as a flame in the mouth of Haumea, the earth-mother goddess. He would have learned how Pele hopped from island to island and expressed her female wrath by causing great eruptions to occur wherever she went.

Even today you'll hear and even observe Pele-related stories. Travelers tell tales about encountering mysterious, white-haired ladies on Big Island roads late at night and miles from nowhere. "It was Pele," they'll say nervously. And local photographers are fond of showing off pictures in which they point out the silhouette or profile of a long-haired, Hawaiian woman they swear is Pele. Another, more typical sight, one that you will experience regularly during or after an eruption, is that of groups of Hawaiian people gathered at the volcano's edge, chanting supplications and making offerings in Pele's name. These pilgrims arrive at the site of a Pele appearance with *hoʻokupu*, or tributes, such as special flower *leis*, sacred *ohelo* berries, taro tops and human hair wrapped in sacred *ti* leaves. But also, in a more contemporary deference to her re-

puted fondness for strong spirits, they will also toss the occasional full bottle of fine gin into her fire.

A prominent Honolulu author recently recounted a charming, personal volcano story that involved the late Hawaiian *hula* dancer Iolani Luahine and a shy National Parks ranger who had recently been assigned to duty at the Volcanoes National Park. At this particular time, during the mid-1970s, the Volcanoes area was being visited by Madame Pele, who was putting on a fiery show that was spectacular, but, according to National Parks policy, also dangerous. To protect visitors from possible injury, trails to the edge of the active crater were cordoned off and volcano-watchers were ordered to stay several hundred yards away from the caldera's hot rim.

As Pele thundered away and spectacular fire fountains exploded into the air, a car came roaring up to the National Parks check point and screeched to a halt a few feet away from the gathered volcano-watchers and that conscientious park ranger. Out of the car bounded Iolani Luahine, a wild-eyed and silver-haired lady who was well known to local folks as one of the finest *hula* dancers, and keepers of ancient Hawaiian traditions, in this century.

"Iolani had arrived bearing offerings for Pele," the author said, "and before the young park ranger knew

Nature's unexpected little wonders regularly attract the attention of visiting botanists and photographers. Such studies include the interior of a low-lying palm plant (left) at Hilo's lush Liliuokalani Gardens, and "caught water" (above) that glows like a piece of uncut crystal in a Waipio Valley taro leaf. This jewel-like water, called *wai'apo* by Hawaiians, was traditionally used in religious ceremonies because it was regarded as pure, having not yet touched the ground.

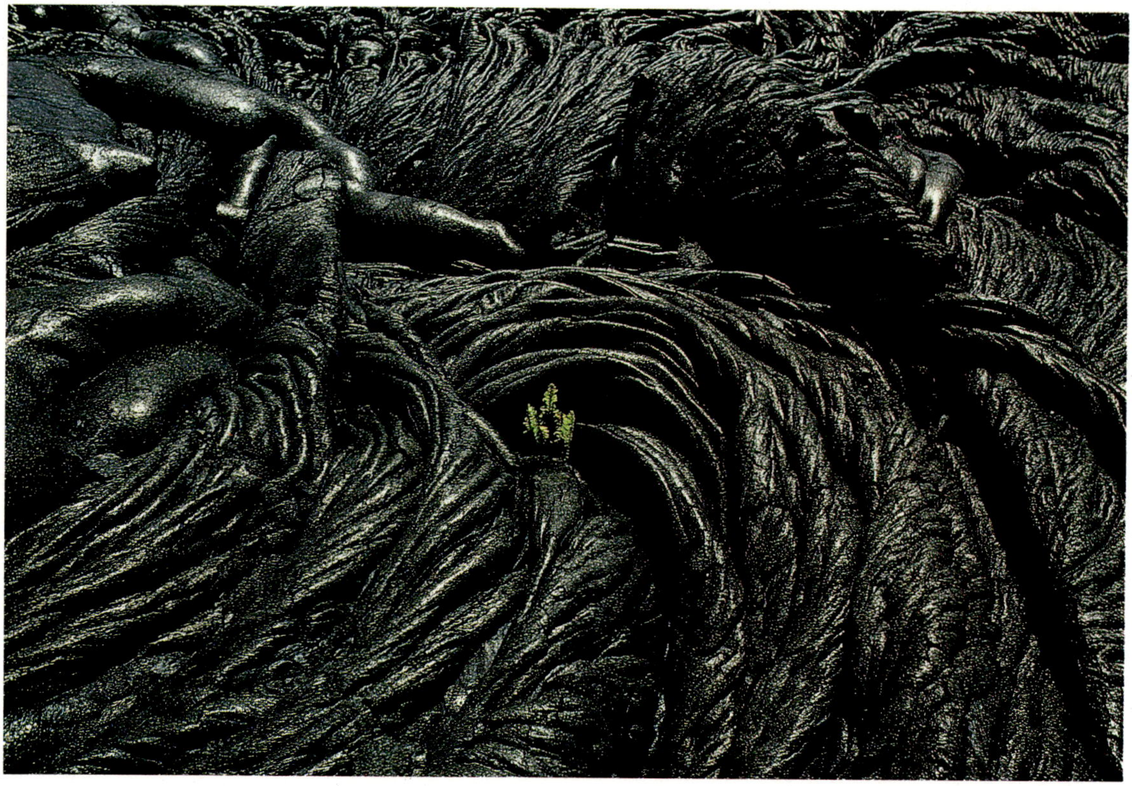

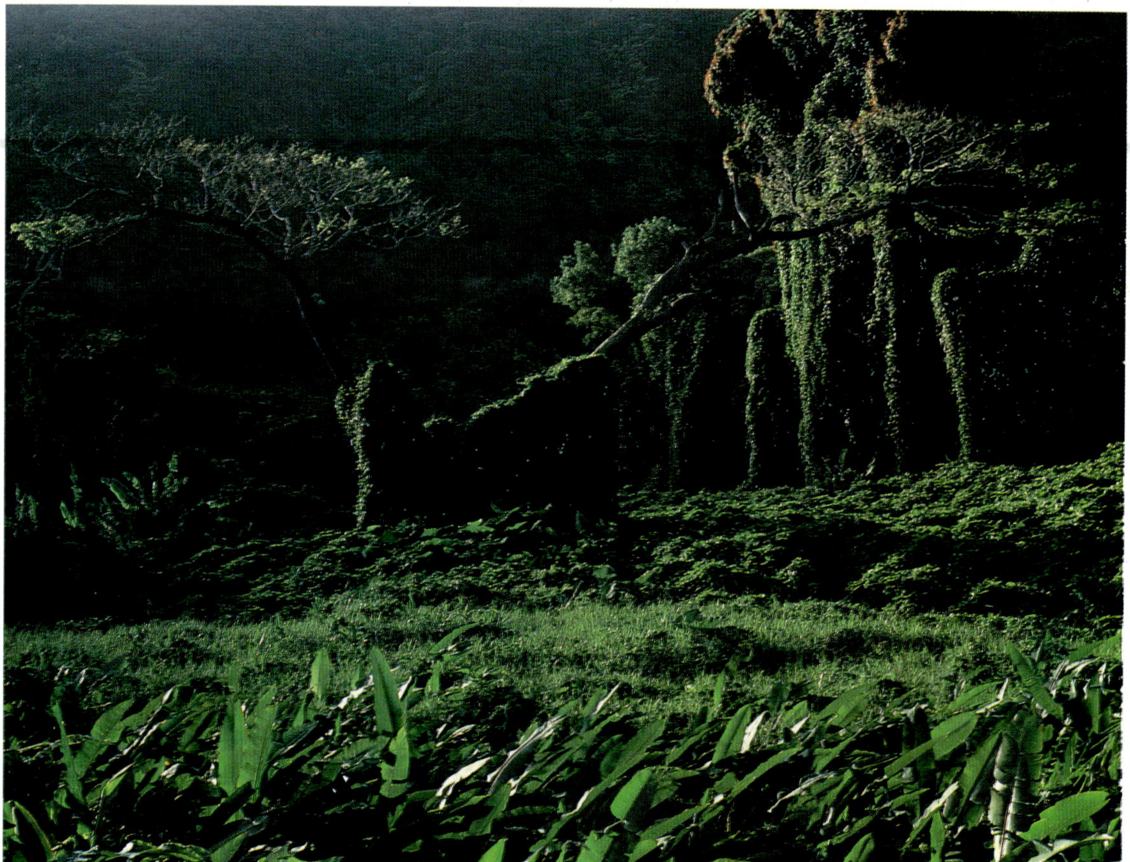

what she was up to, she had pushed her way through the crowd, climbed over the roadblock, and was running toward the fiery crater. The park ranger was shocked that somebody was so blatantly disobeying his orders, so he ran after her, calling, 'Excuse me, ma'am. Just a minute. You know you're not supposed to...' but before he could finish his sentence, she had begun shouting out an eerie, spine-tingling Hawaiian chant and had broken into an impulsive and ancient *hula* in Pele's honor. It was as if she were possessed, and the park ranger just stopped in his tracks and stood there, completely awestruck by her powerful performance. I think he was simply frightened, and didn't know quite what to do in such a situation. He was culture shocked and frozen in another Hawaiian time, as we all were."

That sort of thing doesn't happen up there very often, but remember that the volcanoes are always your best starting point in an exploration of Hawaii. This is because they are—both traditionally and realistically—the primary reason that this place exists. Not too unlike that huge volcanic sphere we call the sun, they are the source and, ultimately, the support system for all indigenous or immigrant life in Hawaii.

Though these swirling cauldrons and flowing rivers of white hot lava initially destroy anything that gets

Hawaii is indeed a "nature trip"—whether in a frozen lava bed (left, top), where a baby fern springs to primeval life, or at the sun-dappled Nuuanu Reservoir on Old Pali Road in the Honolulu area (left, bottom), or on the wet and jade green Hamakua Coast (above).

Even grey and misty Hawaii "images" have a special and subtle life. Consider a fog-shrouded *ohia* tree (above) on the slopes of the Big Island's Mt. Hualalai; a flock of wandering tattlers (top right) spotted near Kauai's Barking Sands beach; or a lone, dancing petroglyph (at bottom right) incised into a sea-washed stone on Maui's picturesque Hana Coast.

near them, they soon cool down and, in a matter of days, begin hosting new and ancient flora and fauna. Indeed, few things in the world of biology are more thought-provoking than the sight of a hardy little fern sprouting from a frozen lava bed that only a few weeks earlier was a seething tributary of hell.

Ron Jett, a Honolulu-based photographer who has made volcano-shooting something of a personal specialty, says that a live volcanic eruption "is such a sensual thing that when you're there, photographing it, you sometimes have to just stop and look at it for a long while. It's so amazing that you just want to forget about working and looking at it through a camera lens.

"I mean, there's just nothing else to compare it to. First you've got the eerie sounds and feelings of the earth trembling under you; then the strong smell of sulphur fumes; and then the heat. And all night long you have this bright red visual just pumping and exploding in front of you. I mean, you know, it's Mother Nature's ultimate show."

Jett recalls Big Island eruption days "when we'd hike across a recent lava flow, stop for a while, then look down and realize that the bottoms of our boots were hot and smoking. And a lot of times the hot cinders blowing around in the wind would begin burning little holes in our clothes ... and making the hair on

our arms curl up . . . and the constant radiant heat from the eruption would even cause blisters to form on our exposed faces and hands. You can get a real bad sunburn out there if you're not careful—even at night."

The volcano, however, can also be a useful phenomenon. Jett has spent cold and rainy nights in the Volcano area when he and other photographers would timidly "edge closer to a lava flow to warm up for a while, one side at a time. And sometimes we'd stop over a hot spot and use the heat to cook up a can of beanie-weinies, or brew coffee. And on really rainy nights when we'd get all wet, we'd wait out the rain, then take off our clothes, lay them over a good hot rock, and let Madame Pele dry 'em for us."

Wherever you walk, drive or fly in Hawaii, you will constantly observe examples of early, middle and late stages of vulcanism and post-vulcanism at work. Following eruptions of varying magnitude, the assorted cinder cones, tuff cones, spatter cones and odd twisting ramparts created by Pele begin collapsing under their weight and the influence of winds, rains and the pounding seashore. Water collects on high, then rushes down to the sea, digs into the porous lava, and begins sculpting waterfall runs, stream beds, deep V-shaped gulches, snaking canyons and broad valleys. Neighboring life soon inhabits these new accommodations and time-

Want to get lost in "South Seas" light? Then walk through a rainbowed little Oahu valley (left top); board an exotic glass-bottomed boat (left bottom) at Lahaina, Maui; then watch the sun rise at Haleakala's "Science City" (above).

Above: Amber *melemele* light ricochets off a snow covered *pu'u* cinder cone atop snow-covered Mauna Kea on the Big Island, while only an hour's drive away, three local boys frolic in that same light on the Big Island's famous black sand beach at sleepy Kaimu.

less biological cycles begin anew. Consequently, Hawaii is one of the few places on earth where you can observe close up all the prehistoric processes that created Earth as we know it. Basic vulcanism, species introduction, evolution — you name it — all are busy and readily available for firsthand study in this mid-Pacific "shoal of time."

Wildlife isn't as plentiful or obvious as in other parts of the world, but what there is out here is enough to inspire mini-safaris into the hinterland. Herds of axis deer run freely on the island of Molokai, and wild boar (for cooking up at a country *luau*) can be found snuffing about on all the islands. And those odd and elongated critters you'll see scurrying nervously across country roads are mongooses, which were introduced to Hawaii from India in the false hope that they would reduce the islands' once burgeoning rat population.

The most spectacular mammal of all, however, is the official Hawaii State Mammal, otherwise known as the humpback whale. These endangered giants can be seen spouting and breaching away in waters off Molokai, Lanai, Kahoolawe and Maui during November through May, when they visit Hawaii to breed and give birth under her romantic *hula* moons. They are a reminder of Pacific whaling days of the early 19th Century, when old Lahaina town on Maui was being visited

by as many as 500 whaling ships—and thousands of raucous, happy-time sailors—every year. Visit Lahaina today and you'll see dozens of trendy—and serious—whale-related shops and museums that recall this colorful era in Hawaii's history.

You won't see giant cockatoos or birds of paradise flapping about in Hawaii's rain forests, but the world's birdwatchers like to visit and log sightings of rare and endangered water birds such as Hawaiian ducks, Laysan ducks, and assorted stilts, coots and gallinules. Or little feathered friends such as the Kauai *o'o'a'a* and *akialoa* (both extremely rare), which in ancient times were prized for their brilliant yellow and red feathers used in the royal feather cloaks worn by Hawaii's *alii* (royalty). Meanwhile, in dry highlands, flocks of handsome *nene* Hawaiian geese are making a population comeback, and if you look closely nearly everywhere you'll invariably spot, as a popular song notes, "one mynah bird in one papaya tree."

Yes, Hawaii is still a grand "nature trip" that is "modern" in spots, but unspoiled in most places and, contrary to popular opinion, generally uninhabited. Just slightly more than a million people actually live here, and they are scattered here and there over six of the eight "major" islands. And of that million-plus population, about 80 per cent are concentrated on the

Hawaii is the world's foremost producer of sugar cane and pineapple. To sample these sweet exports before they leave Hawaii, visit one of the Island's many active plantation towns. Good places to start are at Pepeekeo on the Hamakua Coast (above), where a field hand runs alongside an early morning cane fire; at West Kauai (top right), where you'll see heavily laden cane trucks like this one rolling down red dirt cane roads; or at Kaumalapau Harbor's loading docks (bottom right), where fresh pineapple from "the world's largest pineapple plantation" leave Lanai for foreign marketplaces and your table.

"business island" of Oahu. By any world demographic standards, the rest of her populated islands are only barely inhabited.

But even on Oahu, the so-called "Gathering Place," you can easily *get away from it all.* Even if you live in one of Honolulu's most urban neighborhoods, you can on any given day, within a matter of 15 or 20 minutes, be lost in a bamboo forest that is thousands of mind miles away from "civilization." Or you can be virtually alone on one of more than 100 fine bathing beaches that appear here and there on any road map (but are rarely visited, even by locals). And if you are a real ingrate, who sneezes at the mere mention of hotels, television sets or rock and roll, there's always the Outer Islands, or "Neighbor Islands" as visitor industry officials like to call them, which are but a 15 minute taxi ride and 30 minute plane flight from Honolulu International Airport. Out there, nature lovers, far from the twang of Waikiki steel guitars and nightly network news, you can soon become one with falling mangoes, 'plashing brooks and others who feel the same way.

Available for exploring on these eight major islands (except on Niihau and Kahoolawe, because the former is privately owned and the latter is a U.S. Navy bombing target) are 6,424 square miles of land, 46 square miles of inland waterways and about 750 miles of

Animate and inanimate life abounds in these isles. Left top: Pilipo Solotario, a former "honorary" mayor of Molokai, feeds a resident giraffe and rhea birds. Left bottom: A Big Island *paniolo* **demonstrates proper Kamuela-style cowboy arts. Above: Petroglyph images, including a curly-tailed dog, frolic on a rocky promontory above Lanai City's pineapple fields.**

Red and green Hawaii visions burst from the bush — as a young pineapple plant shoot (at left, top), a double ginger (left, bottom), and as a lone cardinal in an urban Nuuanu thicket (right). Above: A Hana-area St. Louis Cardinals baseball fan squints at his mascot.

38

mostly spectacular coastline. Interested in specific geographical superlatives? Then check out the highest peak (Mauna Kea on the Big Island, 13,796 feet above sea level), the longest stream (Kaukonahua, which runs 33 miles from Wahiawa to Haleiwa on Oahu), the biggest lake (841 acre Halalii Lake on the south side of the "Forbidden Island" of Niihau) or the highest named waterfall (Kahiwa Falls, which drops 1,700 feet down a cliff face on the northeast coast of Molokai). And if you just want to get cool and wet, sit in a rain forest atop Mt. Waialeale (Kauai's highest peak — at 5,080 feet — and, with a mean annual rainfall of 476 inches, probably the wettest place on earth).

Don't mind the superlatives, brah, because local folk are fond of telling you about such things. They are proud of bragging that little ol' Hawaii — way out here in the blue beyond — is home of the biggest pineapple, sugar and macadamia plantations in the world...and the biggest privately-owned cattle ranch in America (the Parker Ranch on the Big Island ... and where you can surf on the world's biggest and most ridable waves ... and where a Kona fisherman (Bart Miller) recently pulled in the biggest fish (a 1,656 pound Pacific blue marlin) ever caught by one angler. Yes, this is a little place by worldwide geographical standards, but nature — and human feelings — run "high."

On following pages: A Parker Ranch gorge carved by running Big Island rains zigzags toward the Kohala mountain range, while on the nearby Hamakua Coast, a group of hikers descend through a fern-covered hillside near Pepeekeo.

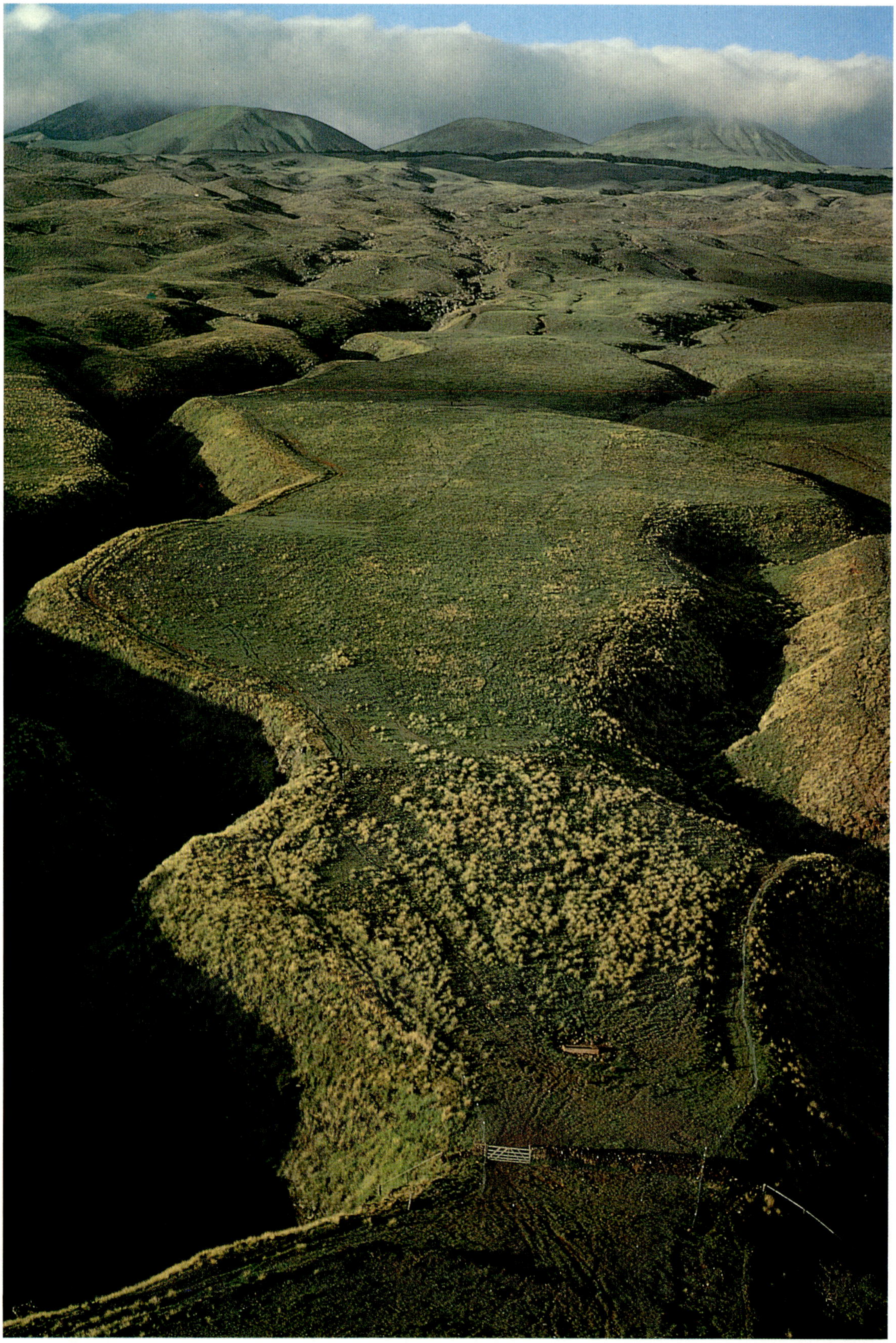

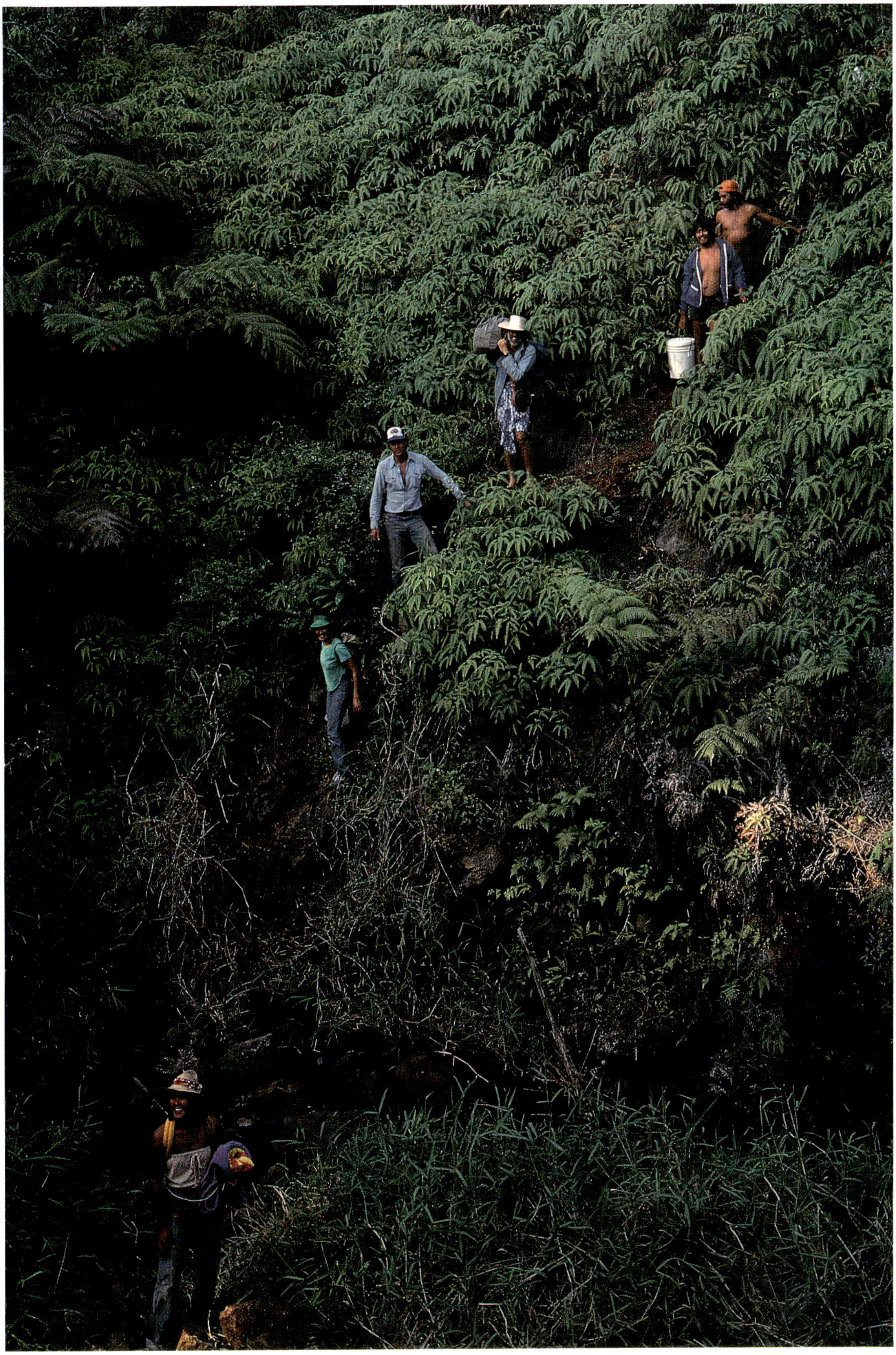

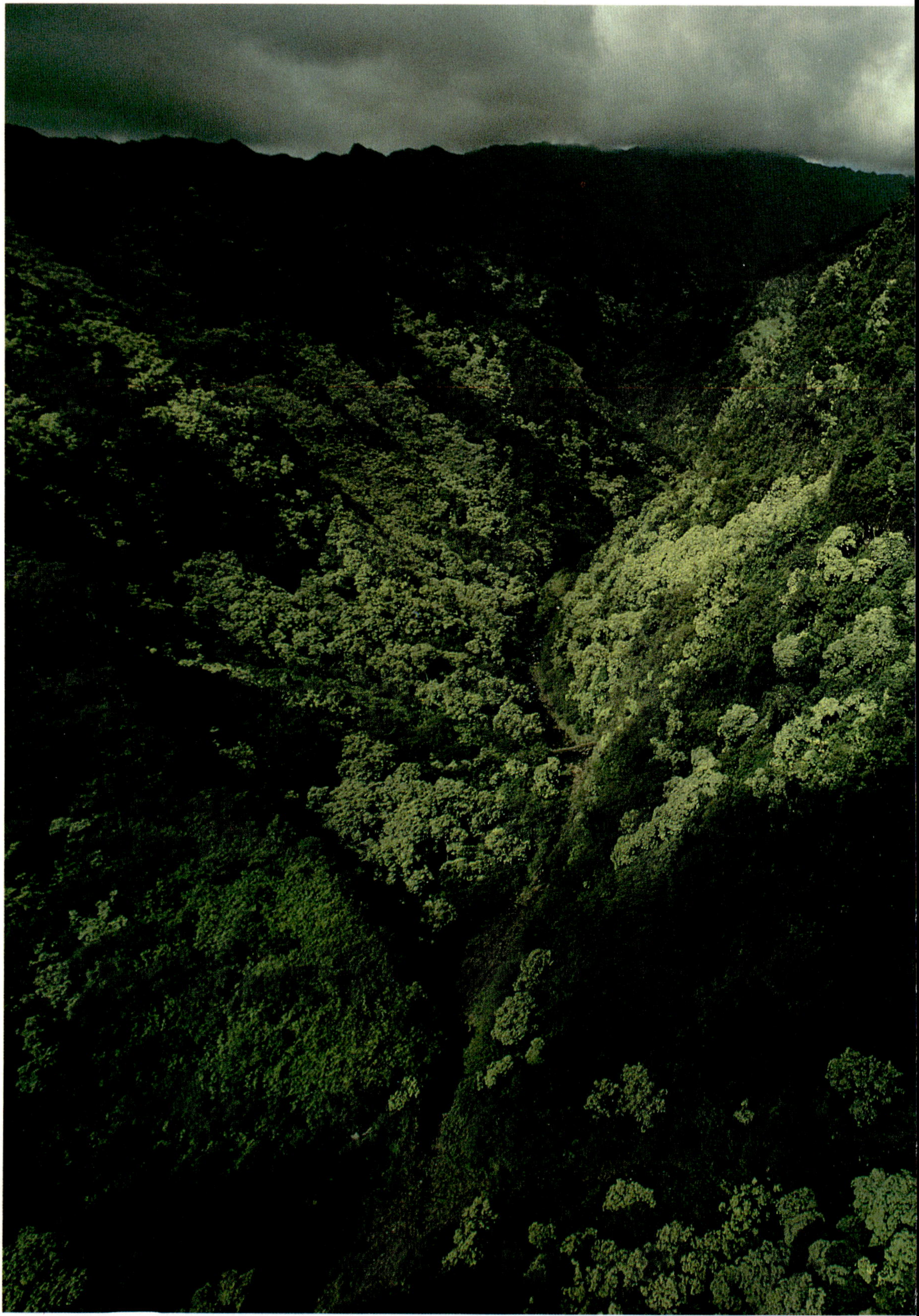

Left: A helicopter sweep of Kauai will treat you to this bird's eye view of spectacular Makawele Falls.
Above: A Kahalu'u (Oahu) resident cares for her plot of sweet, wet-land taro. On following pages: When Big Island winds blow hard, sandalwood tree blossoms called *hutu* blanket Hilo-area backyards and roadways (pages 44-45). Meanwhile (on pages 46-47), a team of Maui fishermen gather their nets at sunset during a *hukilau* feast on an East Maui beach.

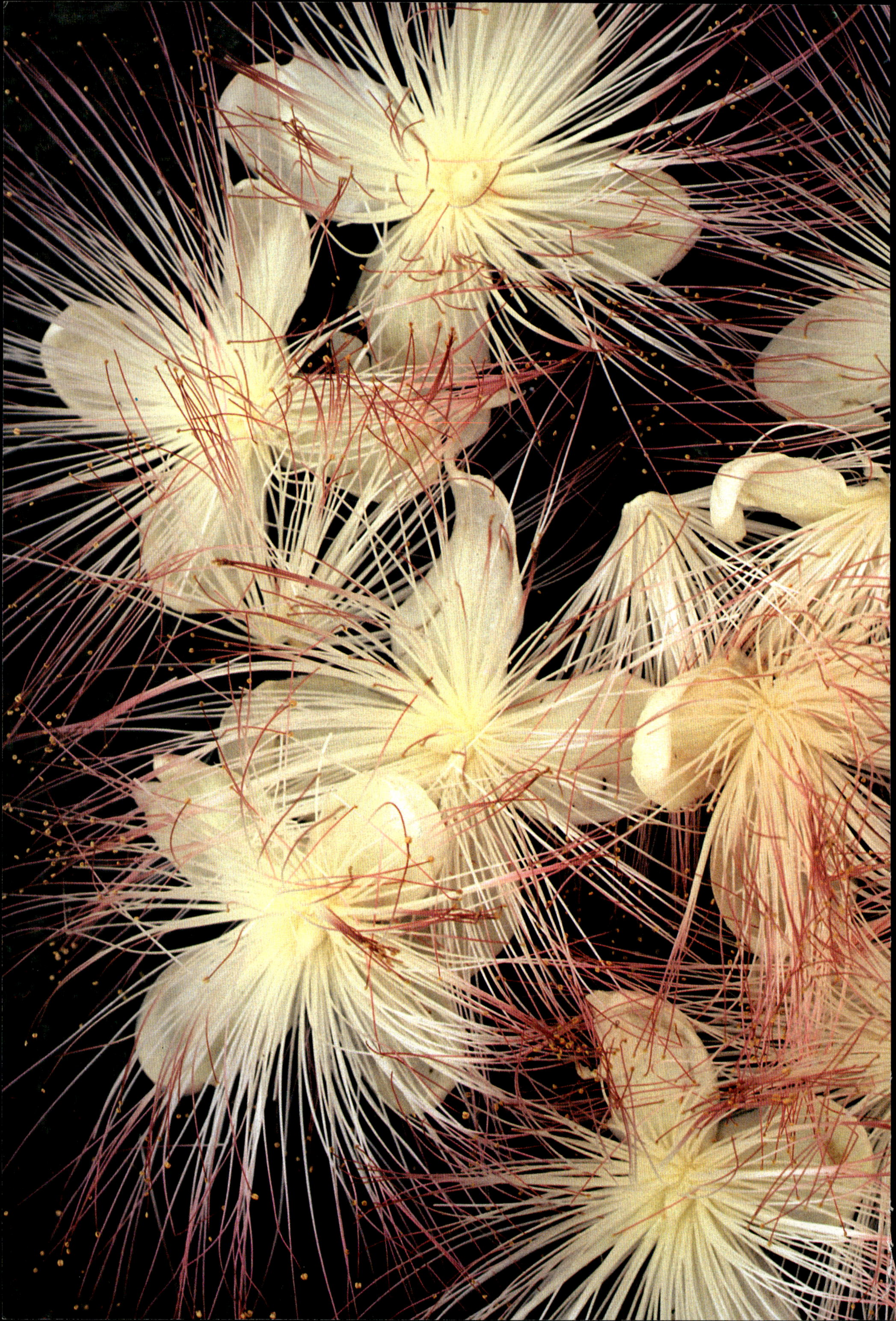

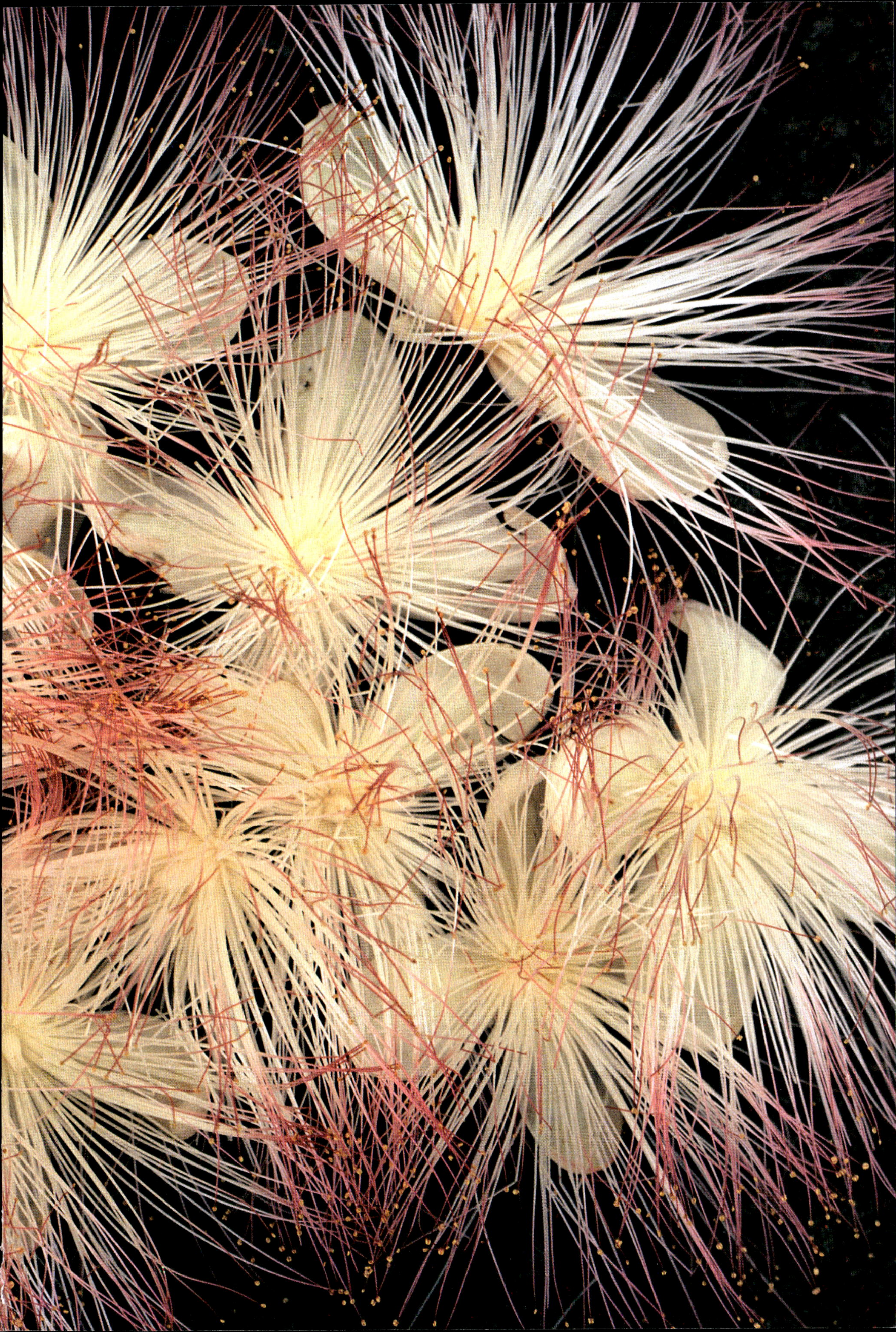

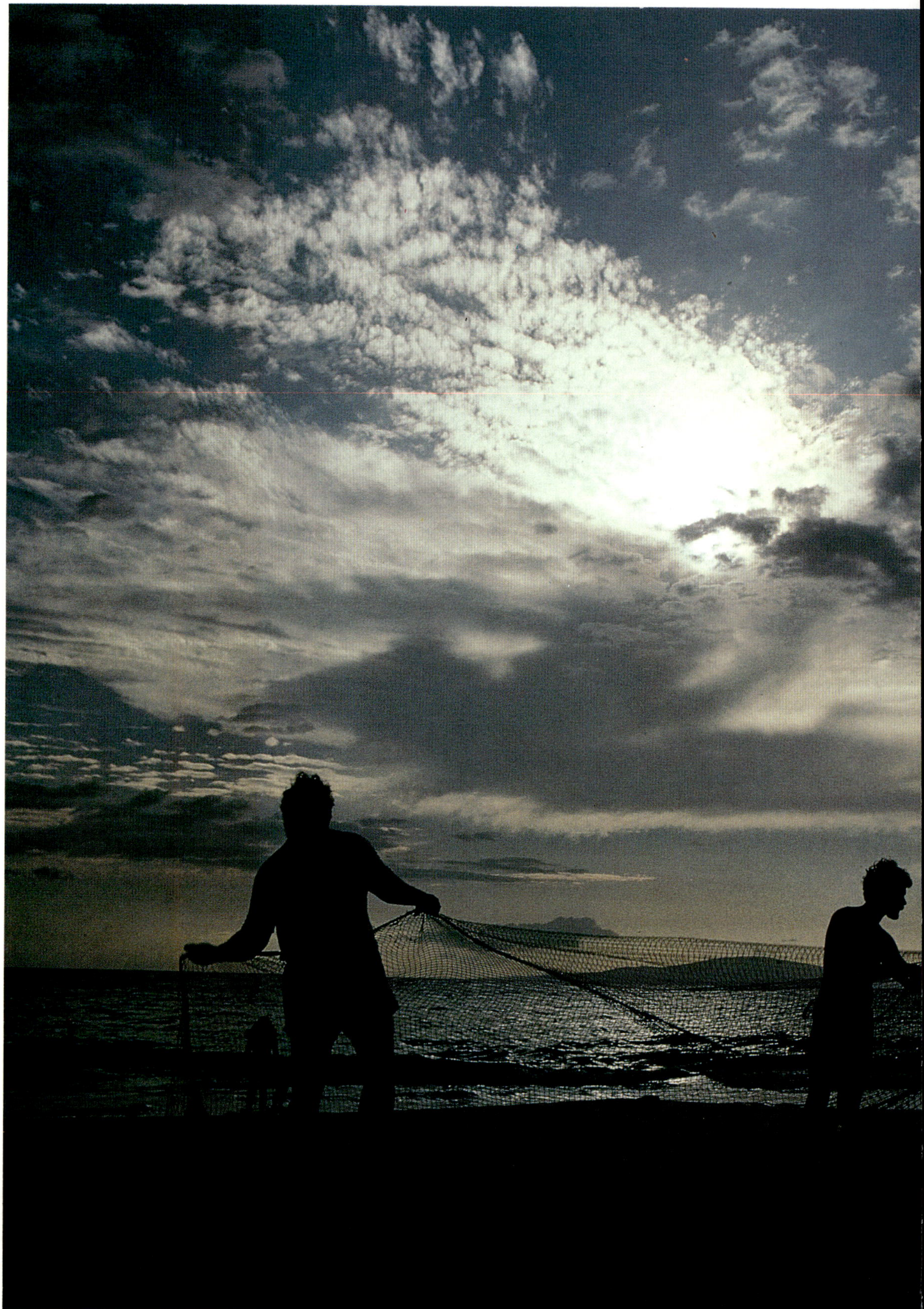

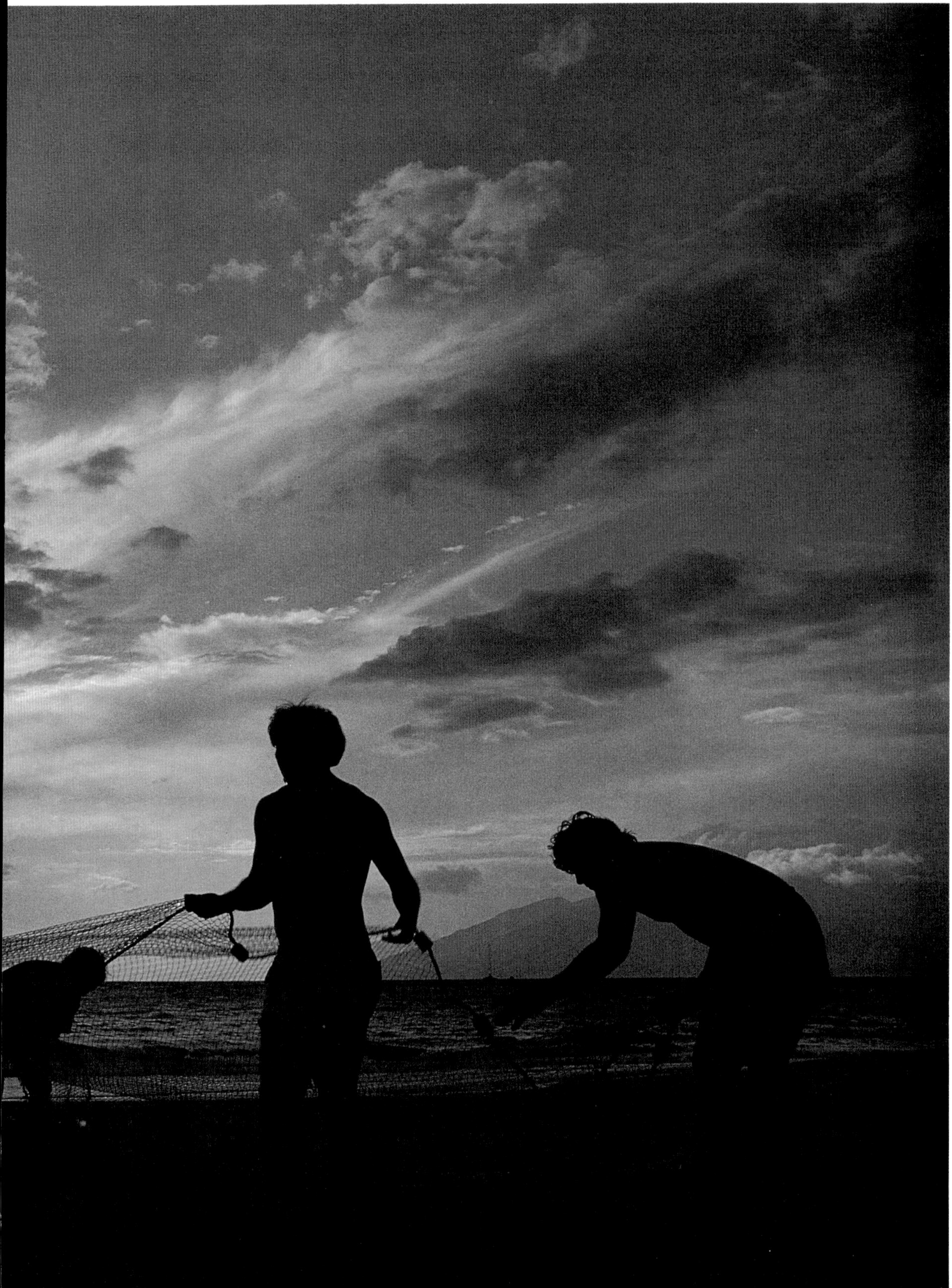

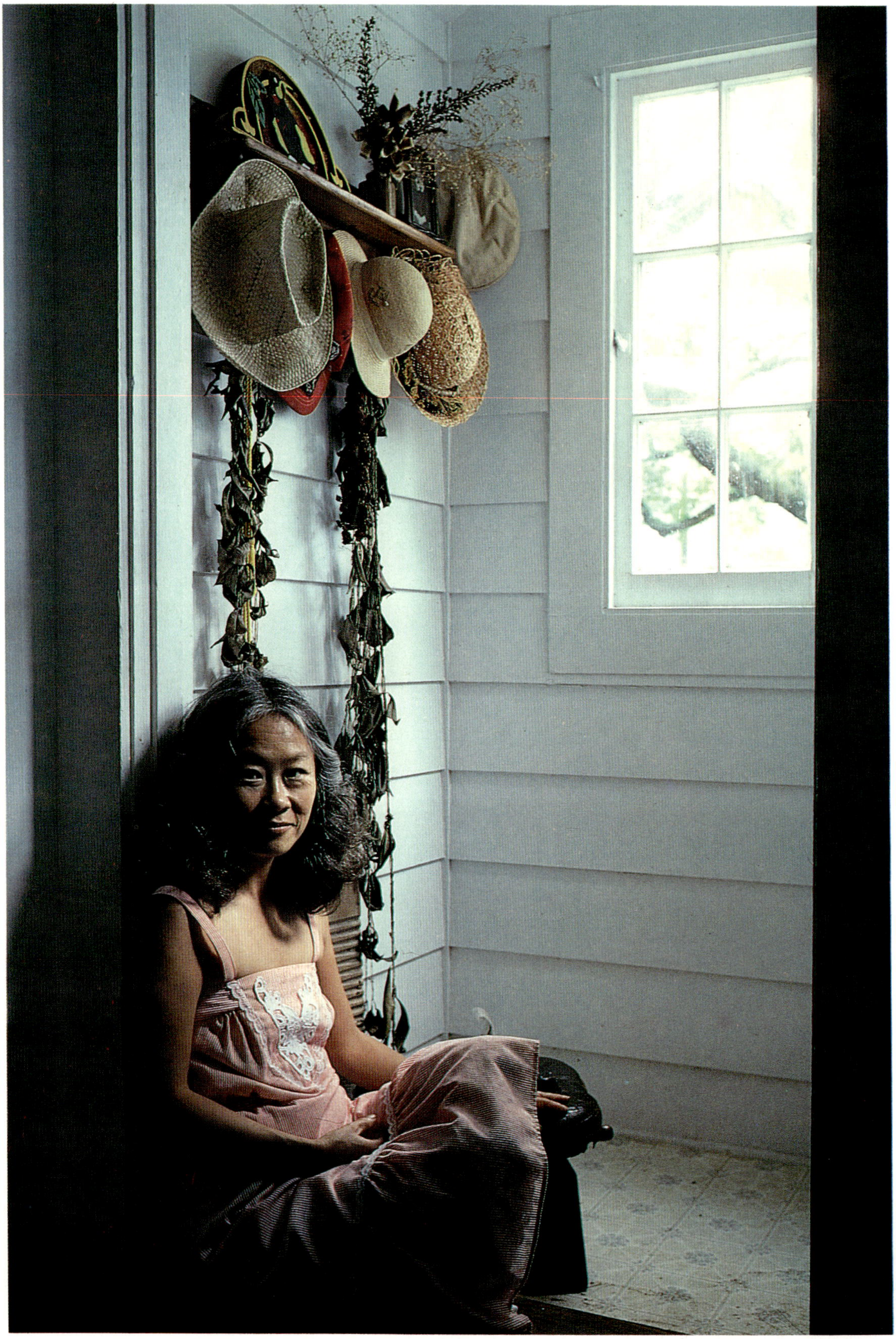

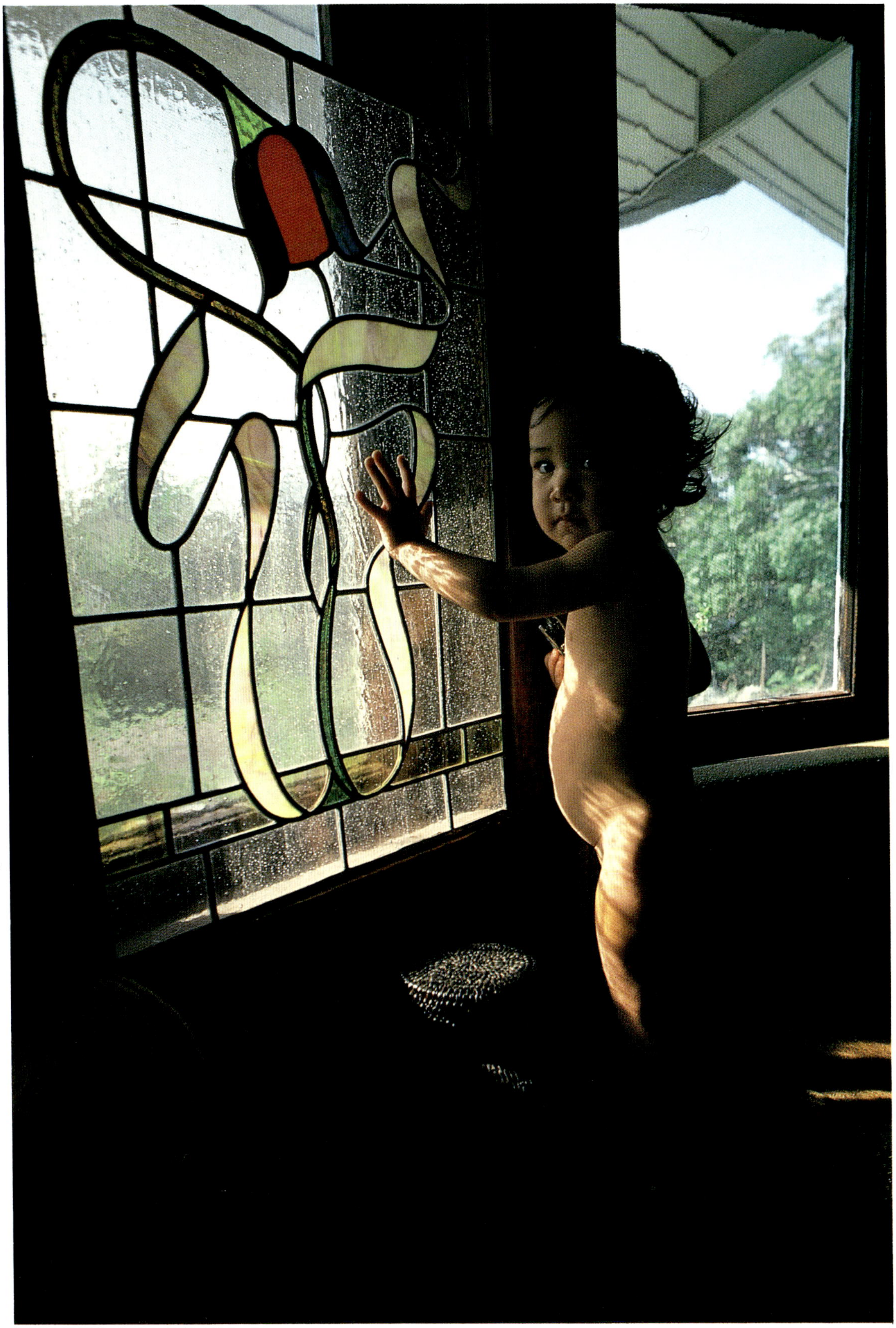

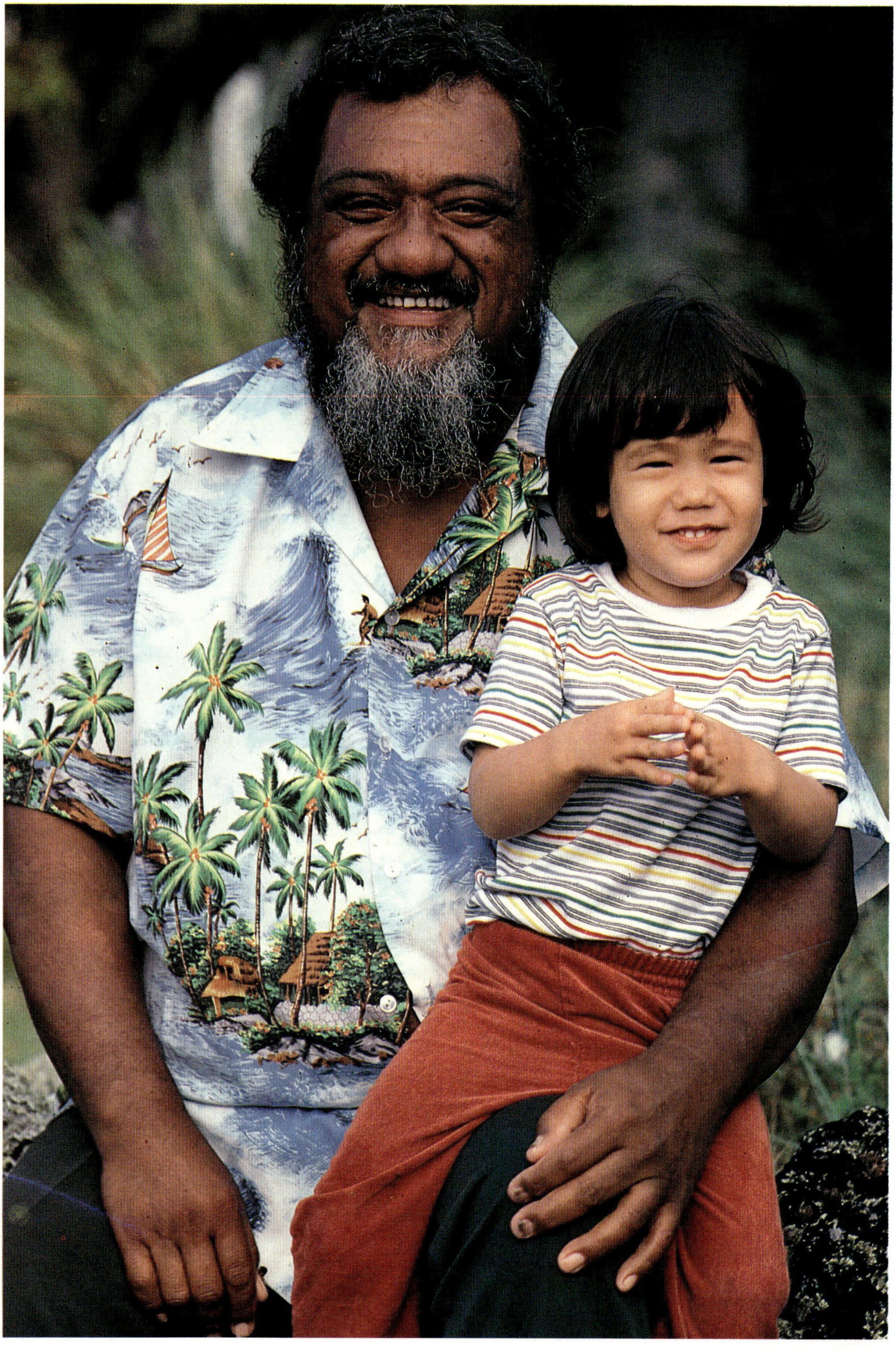

Bore off and made all sail for the Coast of China, and soon lost sight of these beautiful isles, The Inhabitants of which appear'd to me to be the happiest people in the world. Indeed there was some thing in them so frank and chearfull that you cou'd not help feeling preposses'd in their favour...

—Notes from Hawaii, recorded in a 1792 journal kept by John Boit, a crewman on board the *Columbia Rediviva*, the first American sailing vessel to circumnavigate the globe.

There's still something rather frank and cheerful about the people who live here, but in the nearly 200 years since Boit and the *Columbia Rediviva* sailed in and out of Hawaii, the social environment has changed considerably. If he could pay a return visit these days, Boit would recognize many of the prominent natural landmarks he and his fellow adventurers mapped and charted, but he'd be completely baffled by Hawaii's people. They are, well, *different*.

When late 18th and early 19th Century ships visited Hawaii, she very much lived up to her popular image as a purely Polynesian paradise. As a vessel rounded a headland and put into port, hundreds of chocolate-skinned aboriginals would paddle out in outrigger canoes and on surfboards to greet the big white-winged vessels manned by strange-looking *haoles*. The Hawaiians would wave *aloha* and gift their foreign guests with flower *leis* and big smiles. And once these visitors reached shore, thousands of men, women and children would crowd round and watch curiously as properly epauletted ship's officers would meet and feast with proud Hawaiian chiefs and retainers wearing fine feather helmets and capes. Gifts would be exchanged and the Hawaiians would chant, dance and display athletic and other cultural skills for the entertainment of the enchanted Westerners.

She was a charming place, indeed, but that was two centuries ago, when Hawaii's original inhabitants were still living in a secluded "Stone Age," and before any Hawaiian had yet been exposed to the White Man's assorted—and oftentimes sordid—new ways of thinking, drinking and interacting. This idyllic bubble, however, soon burst, and the Hawaiian people found themselves falling, uncontrollably, into a cultural abyss. For openers, previously unknown (to Hawaiians) diseases—both minor and major types—ravaged the long isolated and thus susceptible islanders. During their first 20 years of contact with the West, their society was weakened and decimated by these new germs.

On preceding pages: Two Manoa maidens pose in that quiet valley's soft window light, while (on facing page and above) smiling local folks pose for an Oahu photographer's pleasure.

From the time of Captain Cook's first visit here in 1778 to the beginning of the 1890s, the Hawaiian population shrank from an estimated 300,000 to a meagre 40,000, or about 13 percent of their original numbers.

Today, largely as a result of those debilitating diseases, but also because the surviving Hawaiians have since married into newer immigrant cultures during the past two centuries, there is a serious dearth of Hawaiians in Hawaii. Some prominent sociologists here believe that not a single *pure* Hawaiian still exists in this place that bears the race's name. Sure, you'll see many Polynesian-looking people here that might look Hawaiian, but they are probably Samoans or, like the predominantly *mestizo* Indians of Mexico, Hawaiian natives of mixed blood.

Consequently, the social scene at today's air and sea ports differs radically from what our man Boit observed in 1792. If you're a first time visitor who knows a local person, or if your tour company has made perfunctory "ah-low-huh" arrangements, you might still receive a flower *lei* greeting, but moments later—as you cruise into town and survey the people whizzing past the tinted windows of your airport-to-Waikiki bus—you may be in for a mild shock. "Can this really be Hawaii?" you'll ask, wondering aloud where all the Hawaiians have gone.

Instead of dark-skinned and garlanded Polynesian warriors and maidens, you will more often than not find yourself in a sea of distinctly Asian faces with Japanese, Chinese, Korean or Filipino names. Or you'll blend into a crowd of good ol' boys and girls just like the ones you left at home. Or you'll notice lots of curious and "miscellaneous" people that are, to the untrained eye, not readily identifiable. These latter folks are representatives of what locals call *hapa* (for half, or mixed) people, and it is in their exotic eyes and ways that you will eventually discover the real Hawaii of today.

What you are actually encountering behind shop windows and outside suburban and country homes are the sons and daughters of Asian and European immigrants who were brought here during the 1800s and the early part of this century to work in the vast agricultural plantations that were established here by the American businessmen (and their descendents and successors) who in 1893 overthrew the physically and politically weakened Kingdom of Hawaii.

Most of these immigrants arrived with a will to work and a desire to earn more money than they ever could in their feudal homelands. They planned to fulfill the terms of three year contracts, and then return home as "rich" men. However, once here—in a beautiful and temperate land early Japanese immigrants

Summertime, and the living in suburban Oahu is easy—at left on 6th Street in Kaimuki, and above in the old sugar plantation town in central Waipahu.

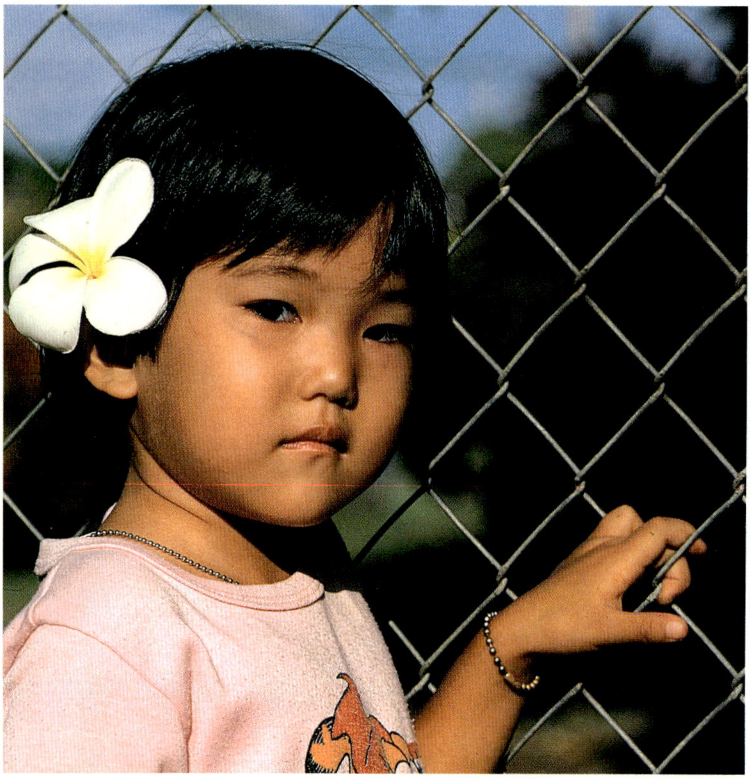

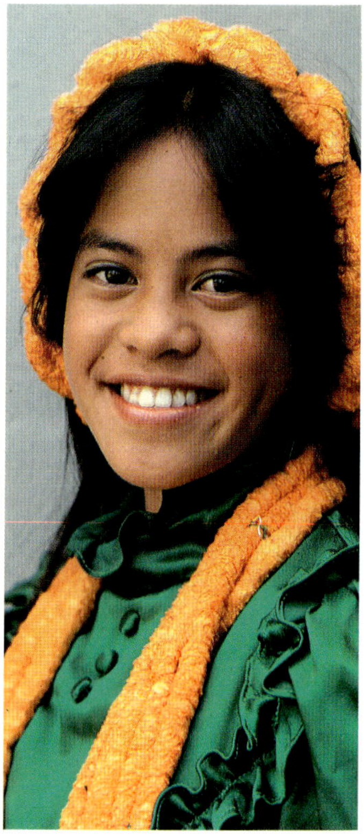

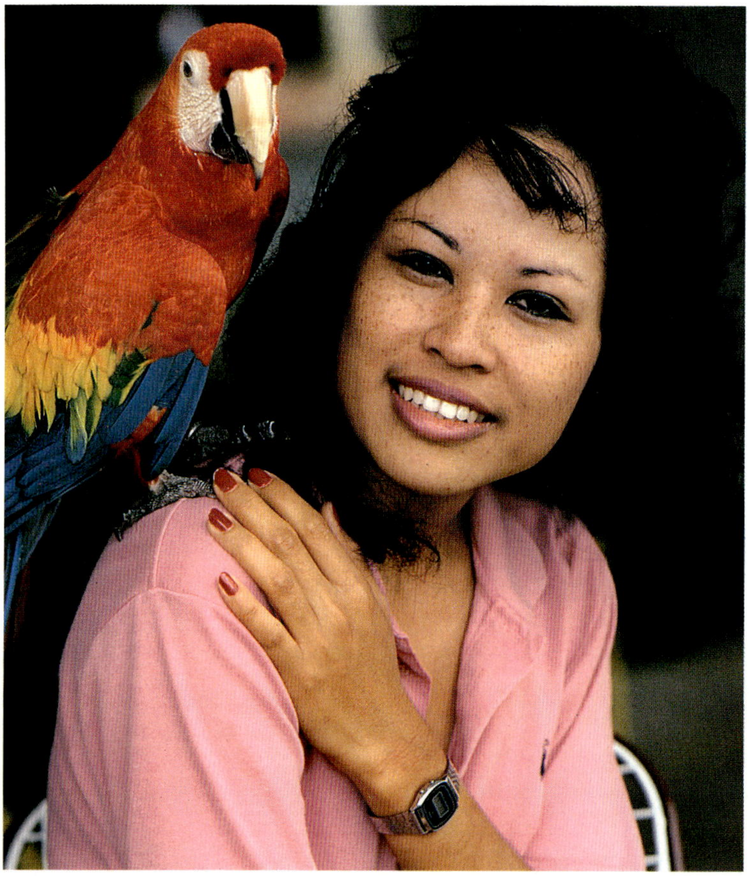

called "Tenjiku," or the "Heavenly Place"—most chose to remain and begin new lives as Hawaiian (and later, American) citizens.

Because the vast majority of these contract workers were men, Hawaii's plantation work camps were largely populated by thousands of lonely and randy bachelors who had to make the best of a decidedly unromantic situation. To assuage their procreative passions, these men either placed an order for a "picture bride" from their homeland, or married outside their race. The former procedure was time-consuming, expensive and a form of matrimonial roulette (because the man had to take a risky, mail-order chance on who his bride would be), so most immigrants chose to marry locally, which usually meant they would court and wed a Hawaiian woman.

It was a tough decision for many of these tradition-bound Asians who opted for local wives, but what has resulted is a grand and futuristic mixing of bloods, customs and lifestyles that has created some of the most socially complex, attractive and exotic-looking people on this planet. "Designer genes," we call the products of these marriages, and these days you often hear first-time visitors wondering aloud: "Why are there so many beautiful and interesting-looking people in Hawaii?"

You'll still stumble across a fair number of "pure"

"Honolulu lady, where'd you get those eyes?" asks the lyrics of a popular local song, and the "local girls" on these pages explain the source of that popular song's insightful inspiration. Try to identify the ethnic origins of these five island-born ladies.

ethnic types around town, but they are usually very recent immigrants (primarily from Korea, Samoa or the Philippines) or second generation immigrants (mostly Japanese and Chinese) who married before, during and shortly after World War II. Since the late 1950s and on into the 1980s, any notion of preserving one's genetic or racial purity in these islands has been tossed into the romantic tradewinds. According to recent Department of Health statistics, the out-marriage rate among local people (meaning the incidence of marriages between men and women of distinctly different races) has risen to about 50 per cent. That means that one out of every two marriages involving island residents is interracial. It's an acculturation figure unmatched by any other population center on earth.

The State's most recent census statistics indicate that of the 1,084,200 people living here in July of 1982, the ethnic breakdown included 26.3 percent Caucasians, 23.5 percent Japanese, 11.2 percent Filipinos, 18.9 percent Hawaiians and part-Hawaiians, 5.1 percent Chinese, 1.3 percent Koreans, 0.7 percent Puerto Ricans, 9.4 percent "mixed" and 1.1 percent "other groups." These figures are somewhat misleading, however, because people of mixed blood often identify themselves arbitrarily or according to the race of their mothers. That's why you shouldn't be surprised if you

Designer genes indeed! Or as sociologists are fond of noting, Hawaii is the only place in America where everyone is a member of a minority group or groups.

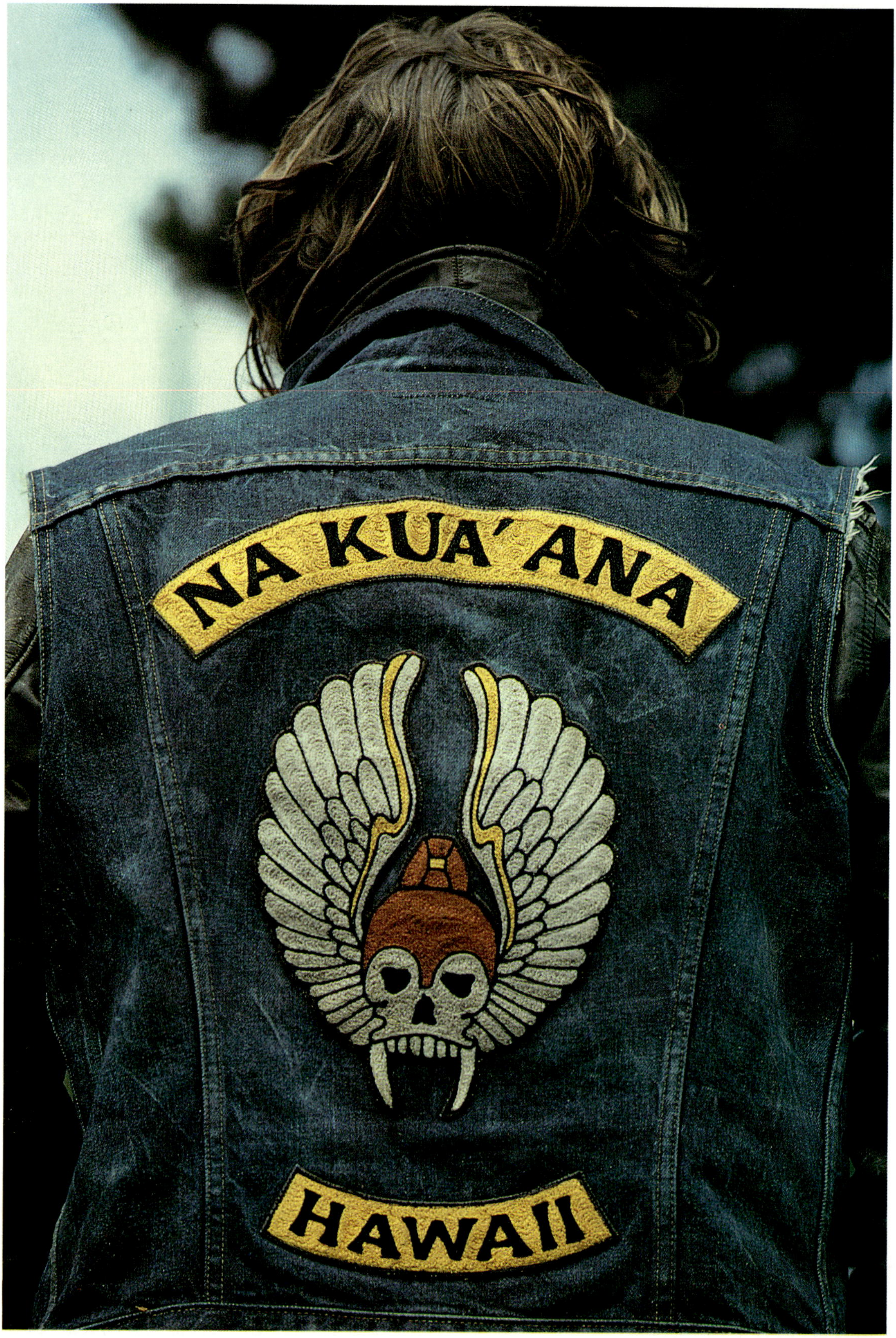
NA KUA'ANA
HAWAII

meet a "Hawaiian" *hula* dancer who goes by the name Snakenberg, Topolinski or Wong, or a striking blue-eyed blonde with a Polynesian surname such as Kanahele, Aluli or Kamakawiwoole.

Flip through the personal listings in the *Oahu Telephone Directory* one day and you'll be even more perplexed. During 1983–1984, the most commonly occurring names (based on measured column inches) were Lee (19.5 inches), Wong (16.5), Young (11.5), Chang (10.5), Chun (9.5), Smith (8.75), Ching (8.5), Kim (8.33), Lum (7.75) and Nakamura (7.5). After a few hours of such trivial analysis, you will understand why a cross-section of foods such as hamburgers, *kim chi, sushi* and *manapua* are listed together on local restaurant menus or are served simultaneously at party buffets.

Whatever their genetic origins, the median age of these "local boys" and "local girls" is (as of 1980) 28.3 years, which makes Hawaii the most youthful state in the union, and their average life expectancy (also as of 1980) was 74.8 years for males and 81.2 years for females, or the longest average lifespan in the United States. Plus, their numbers include more doctors, attorneys and millionaires per capita than any other place in the country. One isn't quite sure what these statistics mean for the future, but, as locals are fond of saying, "Lucky you live Hawaii."

These portraits of touring bikers were shot at quaint Kamuela town in the heart of the Big Island's cattle-raising ranch country.

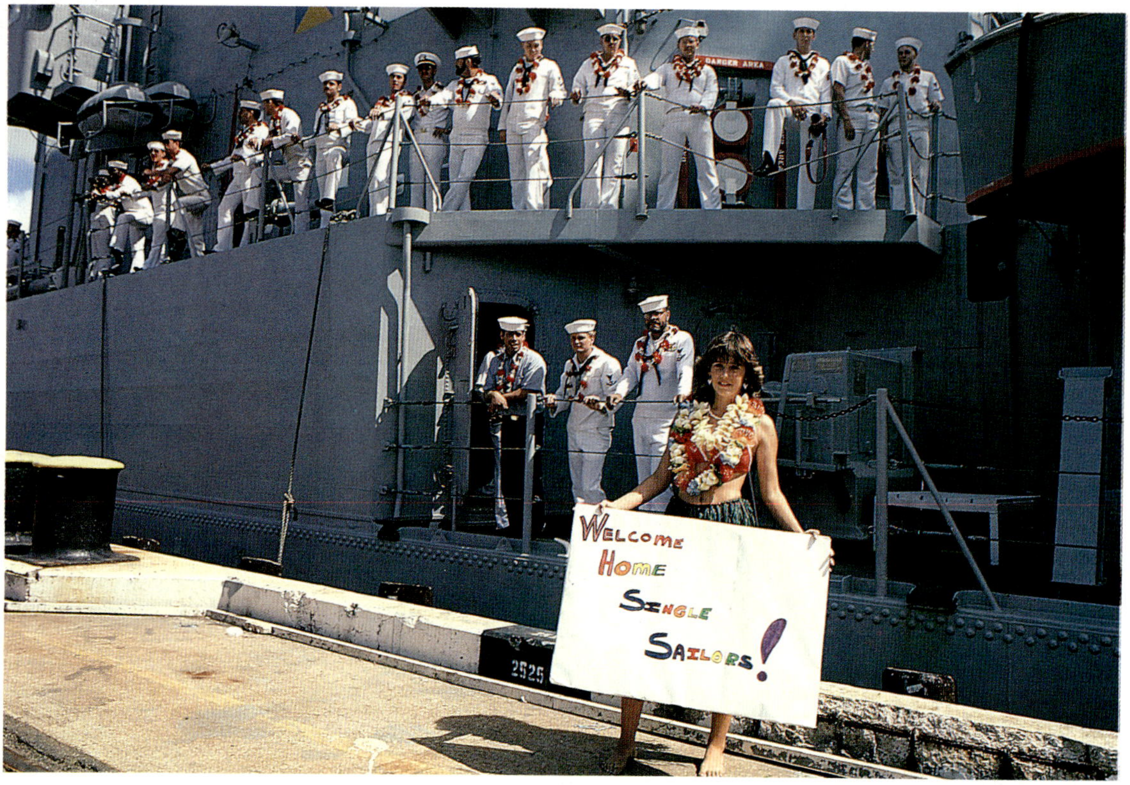
WELCOME
HOME
SINGLE
SAILORS!

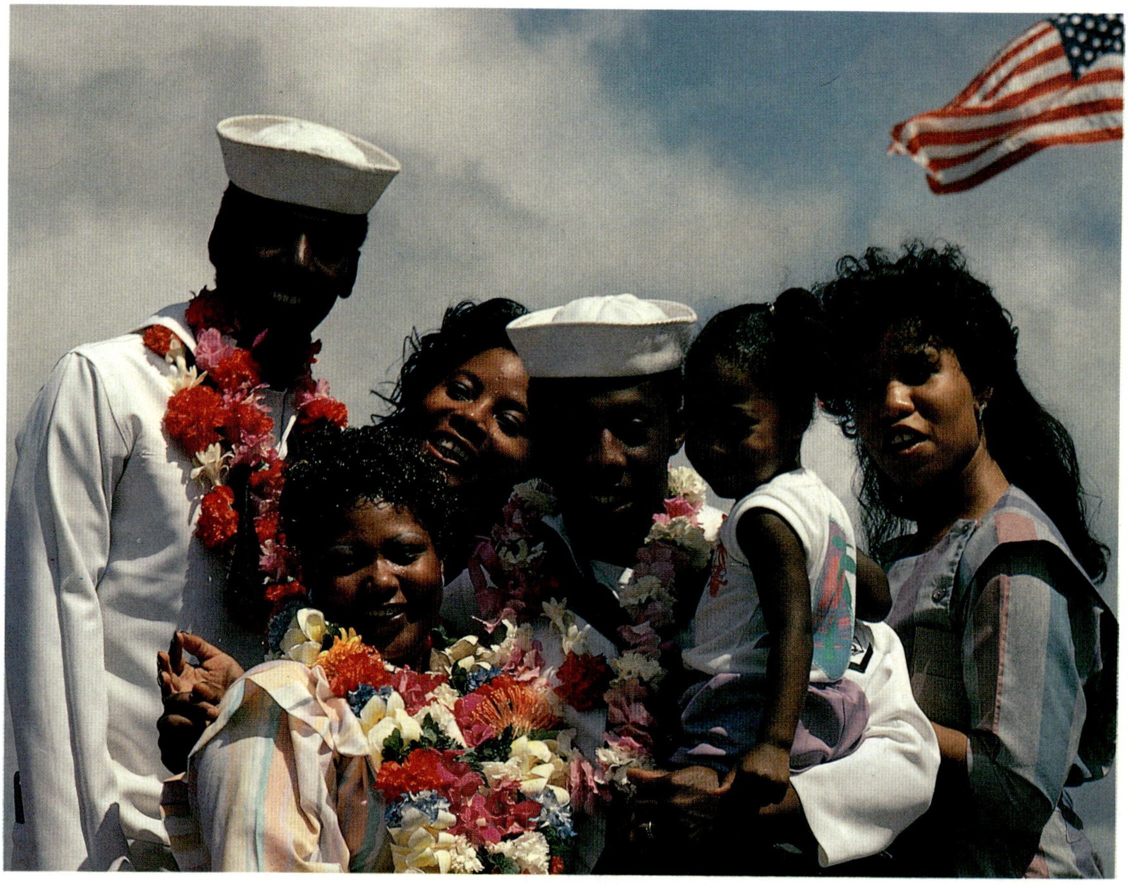

As of 1983, some 125,273 military personnel and their dependents were living or were stationed in Hawaii. The happy sailors on these pages were photographed at Pearl Harbor moments after they had returned to the Islands from an extended cruise of the Pacific-Asia military region overseen by Pearl Harbor's Commander-in-Chief of Pacific-based armed forces. On following pages: Island chiefs and warriors of another era pose on the steps of Iolani Palace during annual Aloha Week festivities.

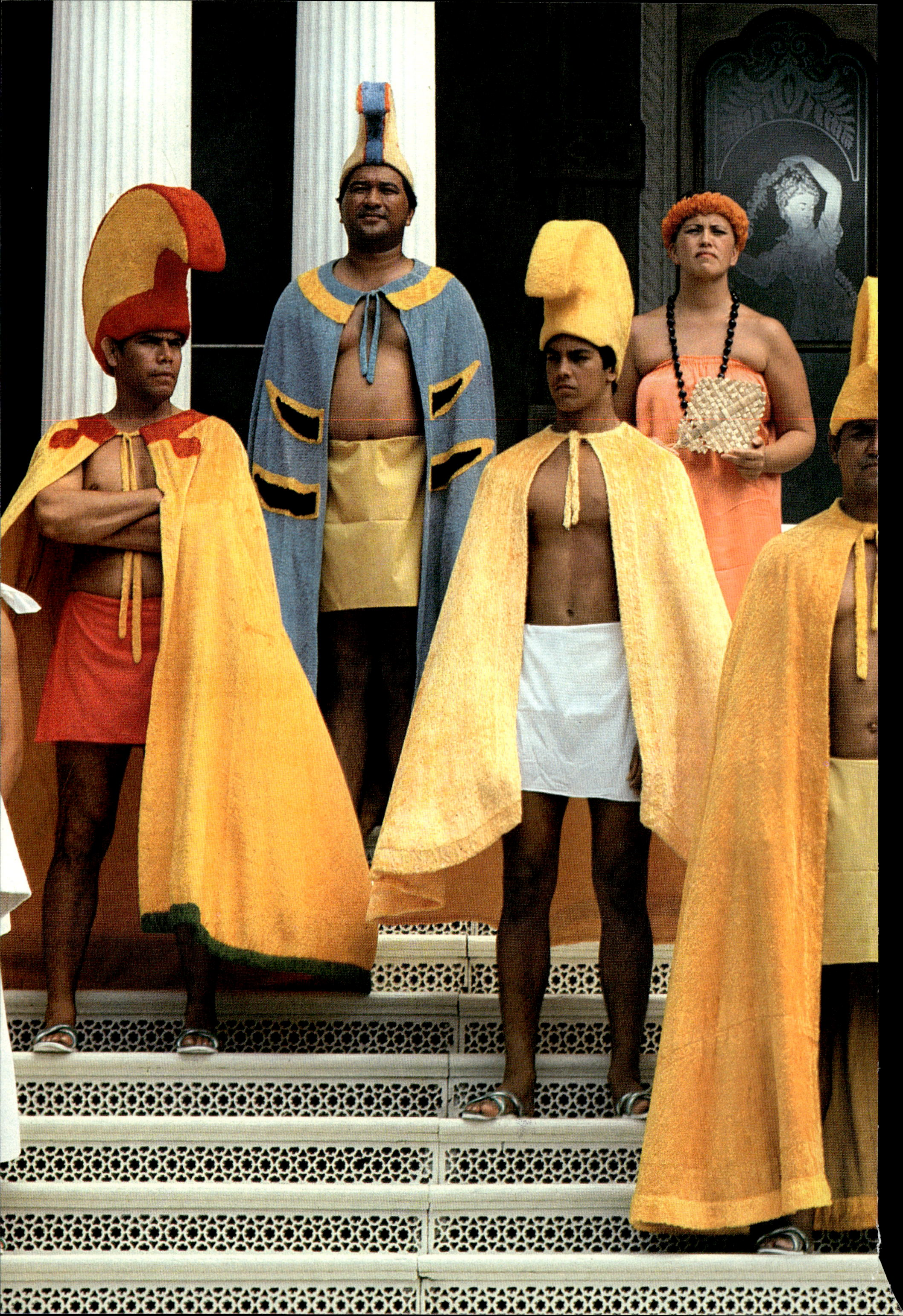

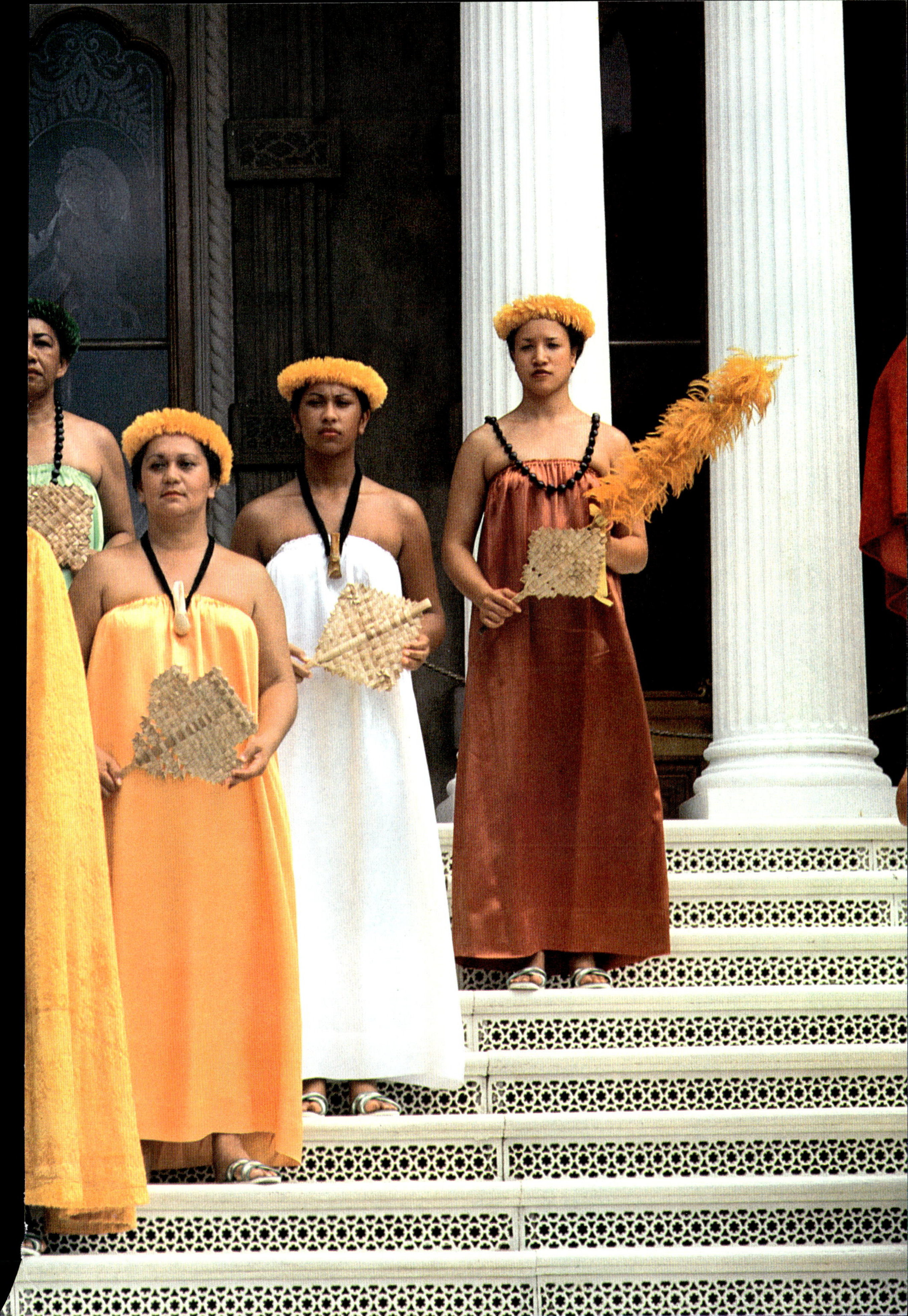

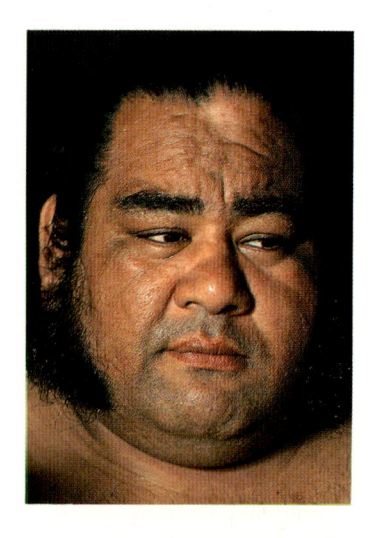

Above: Takamiyama (Jesse Kuhaulua), a local boy from Maui who went to Japan in 1964 and became the most famous "foreigner" to ever participate in the uniquely Japanese sport of sumo-wrestling, recently retired, but he came home to treat local fans to one last demonstration of his now-legendary sumo skills. At the same time, however, he oversaw the debut of another island boy turned sumo wrestler. Takamiyama's protégé is Salevaa Atisanoe, a Samoan sumo convert who is already well-known in Japan as Konishiki, or "The Wolf."
Right: In his debut at Honolulu's Neal S. Blaisdell Center, the young Konishiki performed for an appreciative hometown audience.
On following pages: Yet another prominent and active Hawaiian ethnic group, the Chinese community, rings in the lunar New Year with dragon dances and parades through Honolulu's downtown "Chinatown."

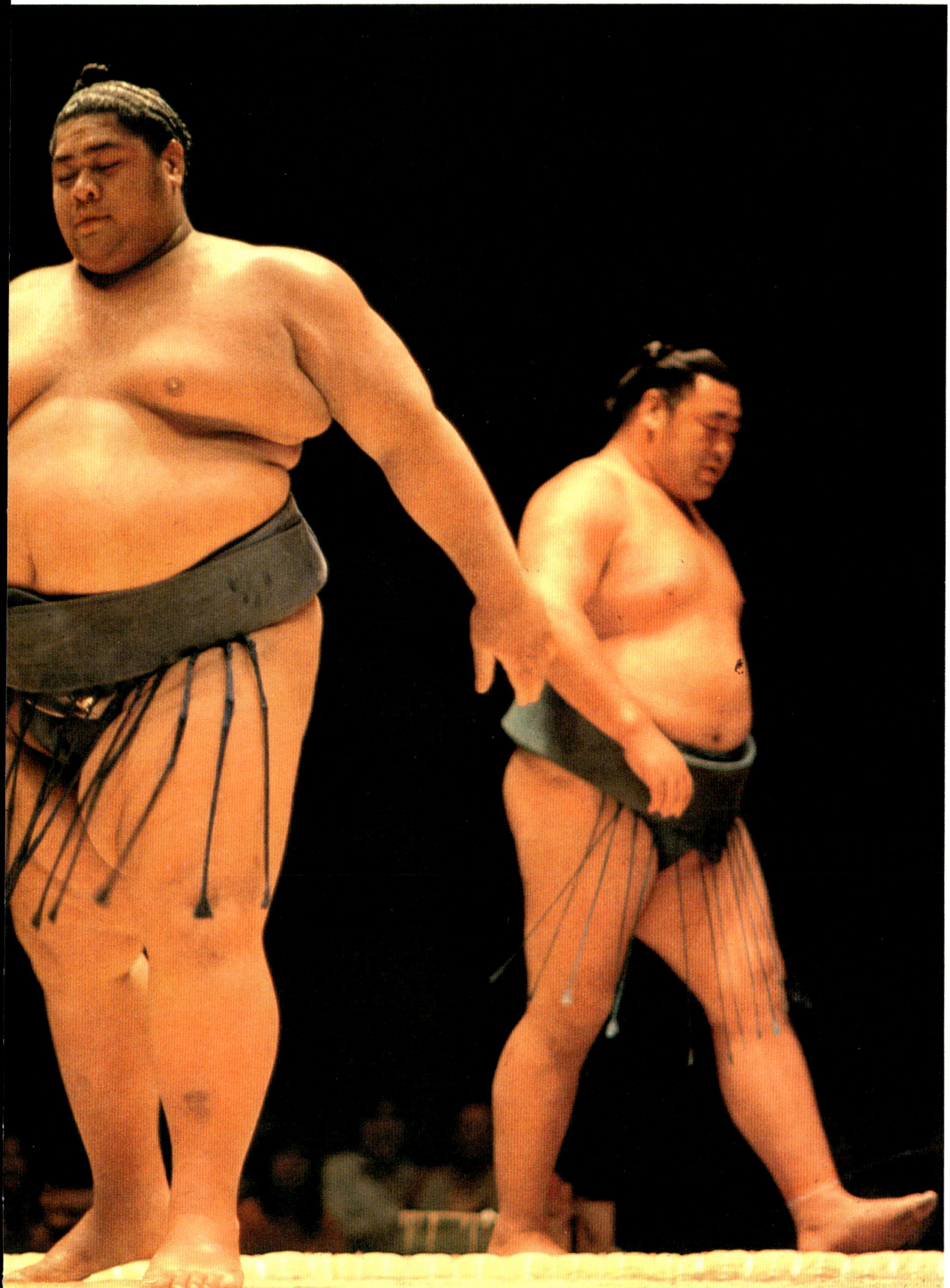

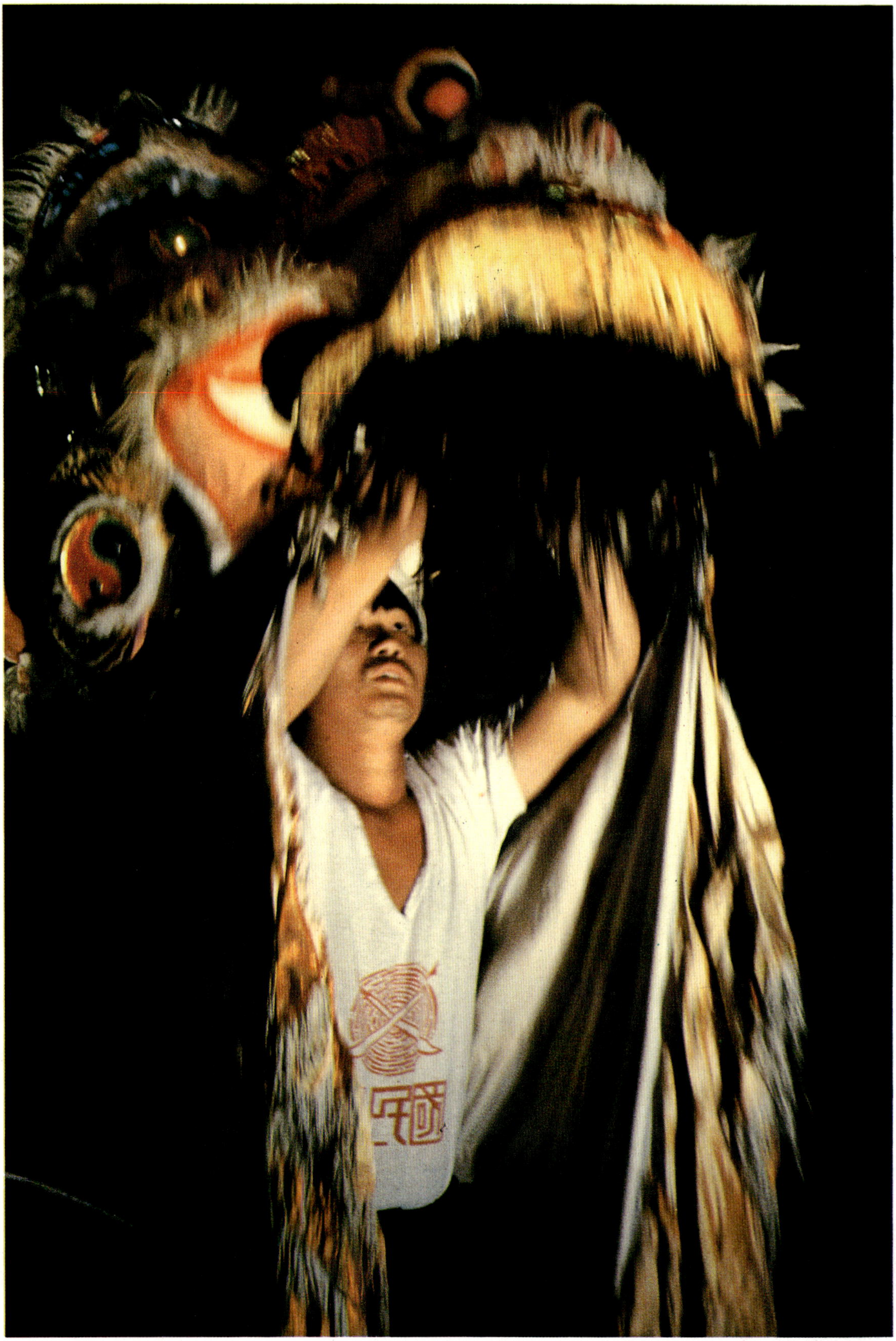

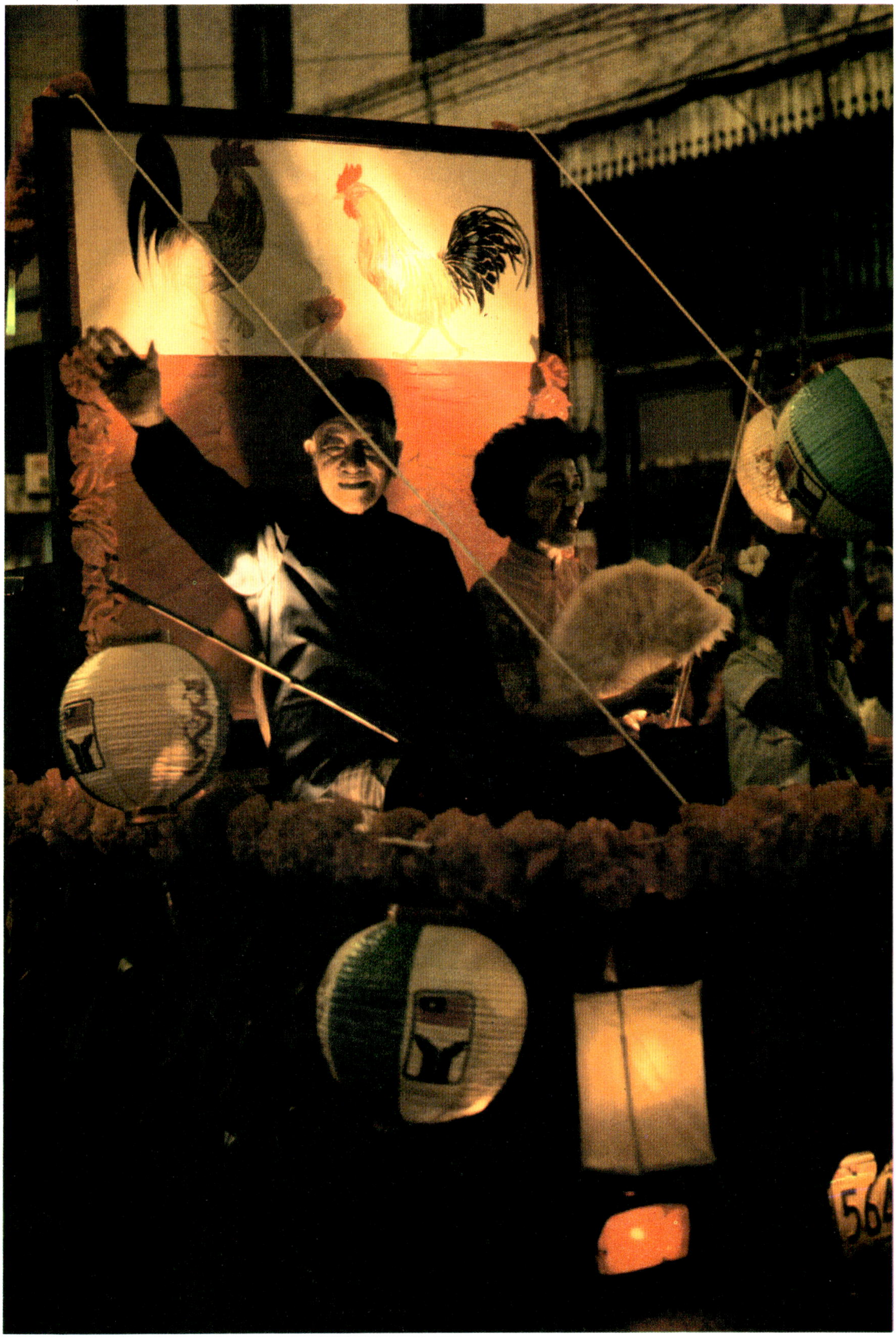

The undertone of every day in Honolulu, the one fact that colors every other, is the place's absolute remove from the rest of the world. Many American cities began remote, but only Honolulu is fated to remain so, and only in Honolulu do the attitudes and institutions born of extreme isolation continue to set the tone of daily life.

—Author Joan Didion, writing in New West *magazine, July, 1980.*

She really is isolated, but government officials and earnest politicians here like to promote sleepy Honolulu as a grand and sophisticated "Crossroads of the Pacific." They regularly extoll her virtues as the world's only true meeting place of East and West, and they predict with confidence that Honolulu will evolve into a major financial and cultural center during the forthcoming "Pacific Century." "We *are* the future," says the senator from Waianae, "and if you want to be part of the action, you better get on board now."

These are fine and futuristic concepts, and this place may yet achieve such status, but as of this writing, a more accurate description would picture Honolulu as a big sprawling town, or a friendly little city in search of a world-class identity.

"Let's be serious," interrupts a barside philosopher. "We all agree that this is a great fun place to hang out in, and it's an excellent blue-green backdrop for doing normal day-to-day business, but what we're really talking about is a place that's mostly GIs, farmers, sons and daughters of farmers, tourists and civil servants. You've got to really look for the so-called intellectuals and power brokers, so forget about that fancy-uppity Big City stuff." After pausing to hear the latest score of an L.A. Dodgers baseball game being broadcast on a nearby television set, he raves on: "You do know," he says, "that 15 percent of the land here is owned by either the Federal and State governments, and 70 percent by big *kamaaina* estates. What, I ask, does that leave for you, me and everybody else?"

That analytical speaker, a know-it-all journalist, is sitting at the Columbia Inn, at the "top" of Honolulu's busy Kapiolani Boulevard, where he and a clutch of local lads are drinking mugs of warm beer and engaging in barside badinage with an Irish mayoral candidate named Bob. "Look," counters Bob, "my chances may never be more than an ice cube in Kilauea Crater, but at least I'm saying something new. Do you want to hear more and more of the same old campaign rhetoric? From the same old political machine? Forever?"

Our gathering of newsmen, p.r. people and locally

Island political campaigns are one of Hawaii's most well-patronized "roadshows." Two recent performers included "anti-campaign money" mayoral candidate Bob Dye, above, and, at right, Her Honor, Eileen Anderson, Mayor of the City and County of Honolulu, at her inauguration.

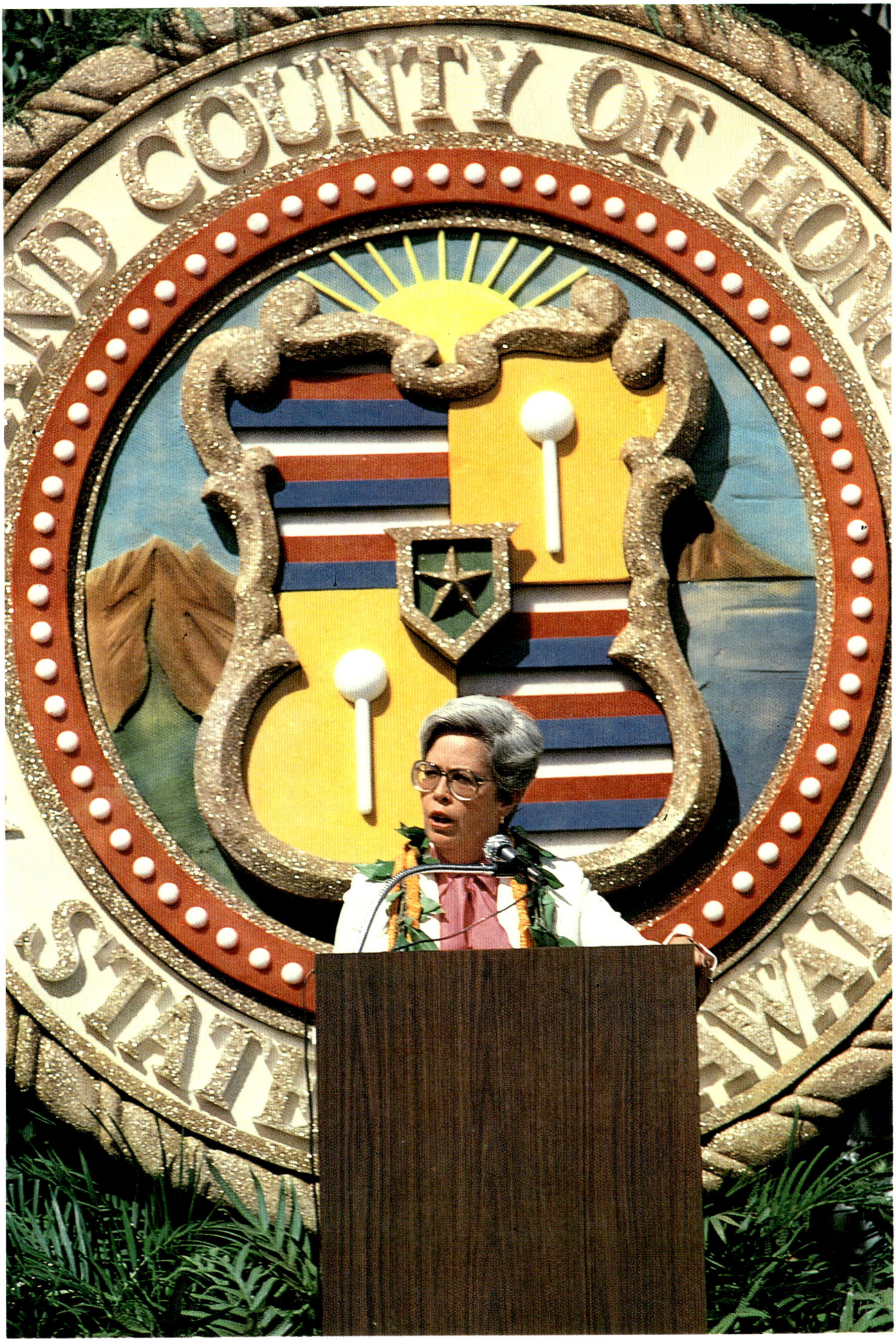
COUNTY OF

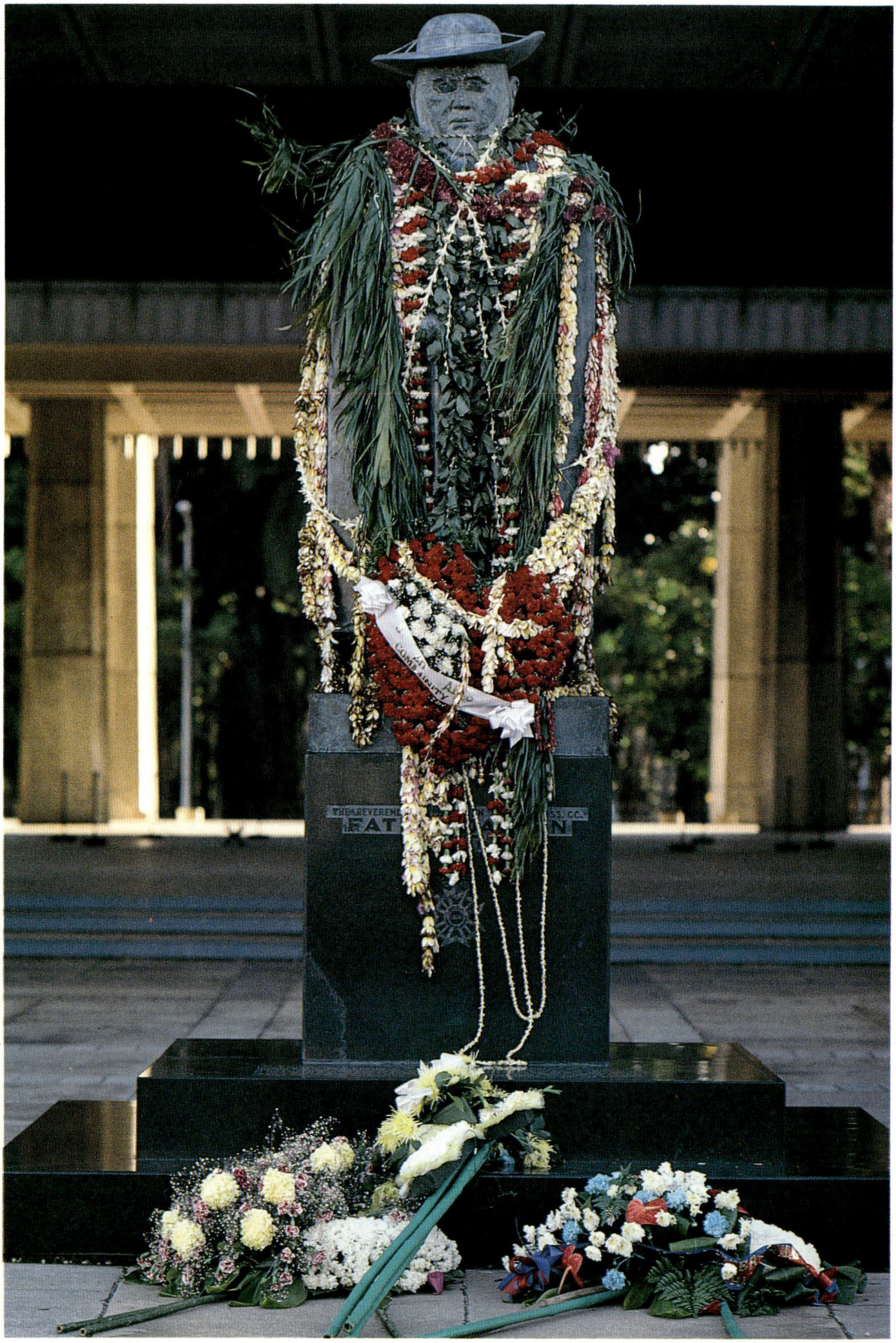

minor celebrities cheer candidate Bob's between innings wisdom, then return to their bloody Kimos, Bud "warmies" and small talk. The Korean sports editor informs the Okinawan barkeep that local Portagee boy Sid Fernandez has just pitched his second major league shutout. He is followed, in ethnic turn, by an expatriate New Zealander, "Edgar the Unsteady" he's called, who eloquently recites his latest lewd limerick—about Minako, who works as a hostess in a Vietnamese bar in Kakaako. Everybody at the round table groans, but before beery Edgar can test float a second "Horny-lulu" limerick, he's interrupted by the Hawaiian waitress, "Peaches," who announces that "the house Mexican, Victor Las Vegas, has just ordered a round of tequilas in honor of today being Cinco de Mayo." A cheer goes up and a rotund attorney known to all assembled as "The Great Barrister Reef" leads the day's regulars in a resounding chorus of "Have-a-tequila," sung, of course, to the kosher strains of "Hava Nagila." "*Hana hou* ("do it again")," yells a man named Puna, and da local beat goes on . . . and on . . . until "last call."

That pubby scene—and its cast of disparate characters—is probably closer to the real East meets West truth of this place, and it is in such congenial interactions that you will find regular and charming reminders of what Honolulu has been, is still, and will

Facing page: This *lei*-smothered statue of the late Father Damien Joseph de Veuster, the Belgian martyr-priest who worked and died among lepers who were isolated at Kalawao on the island of Molokai, stares towards Oahu's mountainous interior from a place of honor on the *mauka* side of Honolulu's State Capitol grounds. Above: Downtown workers talk and relax under the scarlet blossoms of a royal poinciana tree that shades the Hawaii State Capitol's Ewa-side greensward.

HULA ICES

HULA SHAVE ICE
HULA ICE CREAM
SUNDAES & POPCORN
featuring....
"BROKE DA MOUTH" FRUIT FRAPPÉS

continue to be. In a word, she's People, with a rainbow-colored and capital P.

When the prominent British author Somerset Maugham visited Honolulu during the course of a 1916 world tour, he observed this town's odd and chop-suey society, and commented: "Though the air is so soft and the sky so blue, you have, I know not why, a feeling of something hotly passionate that beats like a throbbing pulse through the crowd." Debunking Kipling's assertion that East is East and West is West, and never the twain shall meet, Maugham wrote that he sensed an "extraordinary vitality" in this true "meeting place of East and West, [where] the very new rubs shoulders with the immeasurably old . . .

"All these strange people," he observed, "live close to each other, with different languages and different thoughts; they believe in different gods and they have different values; two passions alone they share, love and hunger."

Good observation, Somerset ol' bean, but if you could only feel the "pulse" and sense that "vitality" now.

Worldly Maugham, an upperclass wanderer who was decidedly more used to colonial societies where Frogs stayed away from Wogs, and where Whites Only were invited over for Sunday tiffins on the verandah, was witnessing the middle chapters of a Polynesian cum

At left and above: Oahu's varied "signs of the times" reflect this island's multi-ethnic consciousness. Such anomalous symbols abound in this most "mixed" of the world's population centers.

loosely Caucasian society which since 1850 has been further populated and cross-pollinated by some 180,000 Japanese, 45,000 Chinese, 17,000 Portuguese and assorted thousands of other Samoans, Koreans, Spaniards, Germans and Poles who came here to work for a while, but, as aforementioned, never left. These thoroughbred immigrants had little in common with one another at the start of their lives in Hawaii, but like different kinds of exotic fish that are tossed into a pleasantly appointed tank, they have since learned how to eat and swim together. And somehow—despite the occasional condescending flap of an ethnic fin—they've managed to maintain a semblance of social order while waving American flags and reciting, in different accents, *The Pledge of Allegiance.* As a retired newspaper editor once commented, "Honolulu is about as American, really, as apple *poi.*"

Indeed, there are other *American* places where various ethnic groups work and play together, but this is the only one where everybody is a member of a minority, and where that minority is more often than not of an Asian-Pacific extraction. "This leaning toward Asia," observes author Didion, "makes Honolulu's relation to the rest of America oblique, and divergent at unexpected points, which is part of the place's great but often hidden eccentricity."

Above: A bevy of gym-shorted "local girls" smile *shaka* smiles from a rococo doorway at Honolulu's McKinley High School. Right: An intermediate school marching band performs for the camera during a recent open-air recital in suburban Moiliili.

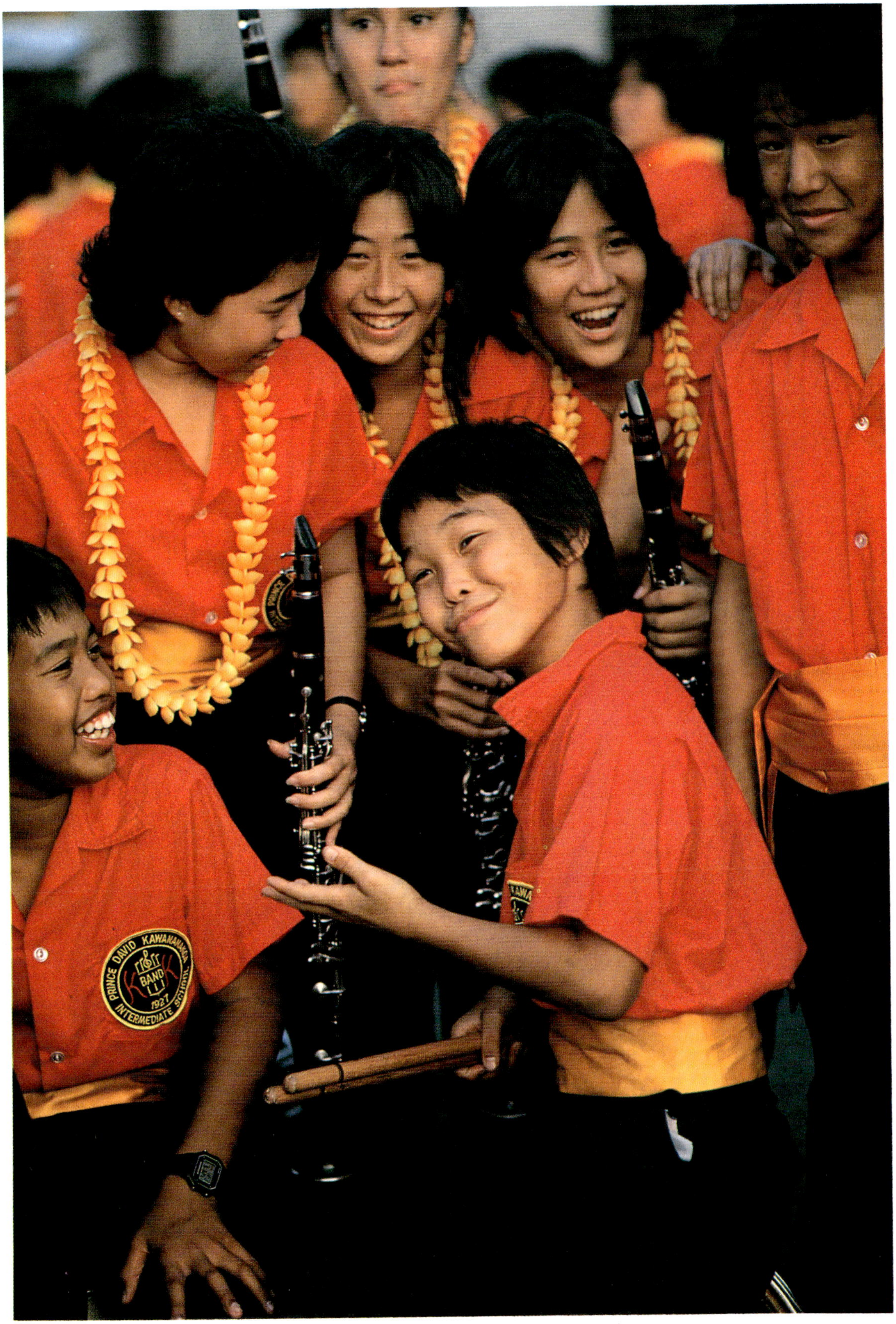
PRINCE DAVID KAWANANAKOA
BAND
1927
INTERMEDIATE SCHOOL

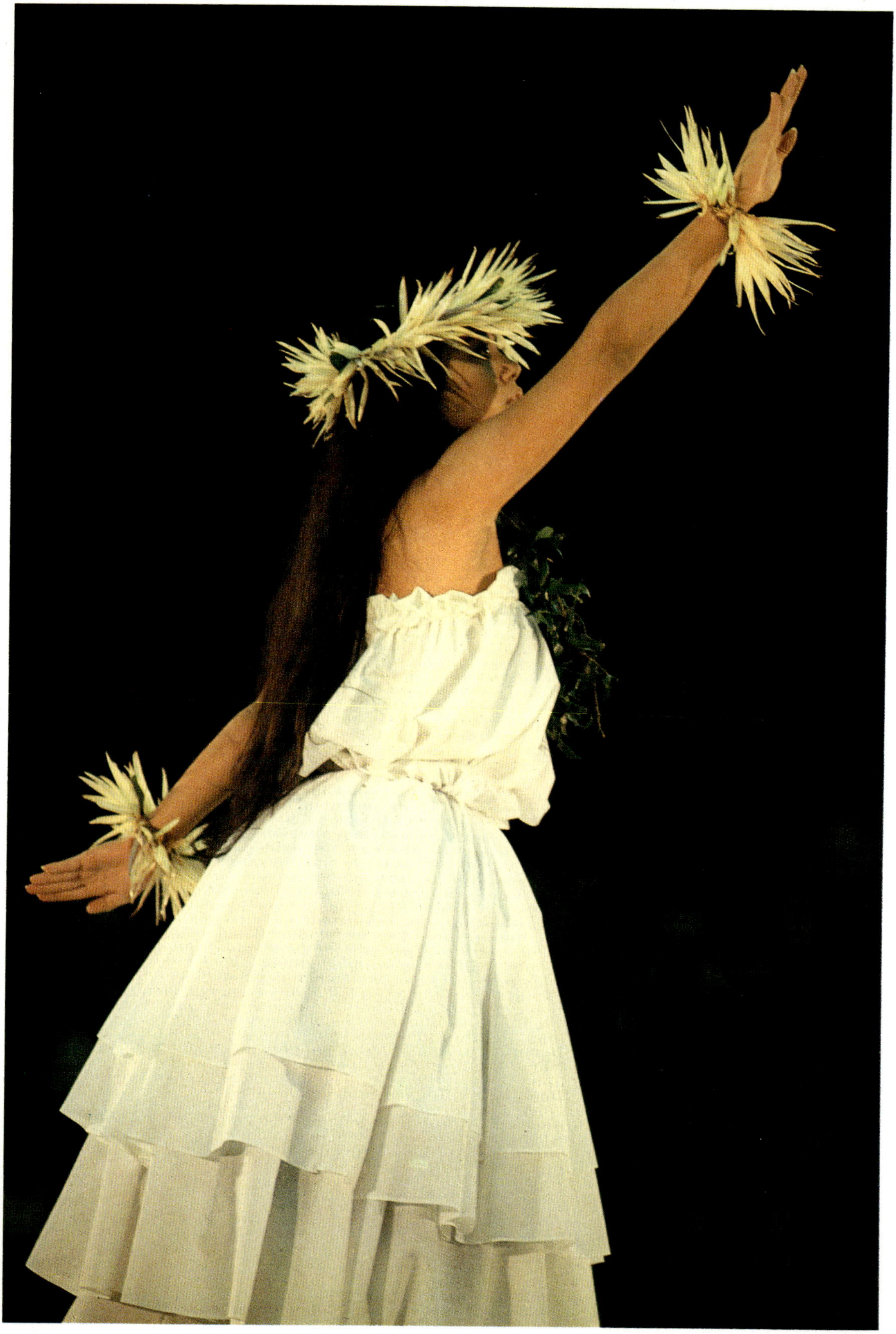

The hula was a religious service in which poetry, music, pantomime and the dance lent themselves, under the form of dramatic art, to the refreshment of men's minds. Its view of life was idyllic, it gave itself to the celebration of those mythical times when gods and goddesses moved on the earth, and men and women were as gods.

— Nathaniel Emerson, writing in
*Unwritten Literature of Hawaii:
The Sacred Songs of the Hula,* 1909.

These days, as young Hawaiian men and women find themselves in the throes of an exciting and creative Hawaiian cultural *renaissance,* the *hula* is all of the above. It is also, as King David Kalakaua once expressed it, a "language of the heart and therefore the heartbeat of the Hawaiian people."

But the traditional *hula,* in its many contemporary forms, is much more than a living reminder of colorful Hawaiian times past. This ancient art form is also an enduring image of Hawaii that is readily and romantically recalled whenever or wherever these islands are mentioned. Indeed, tell a European or Asian person that you're from Hawaii, and the first thing he or she says is "*hula-hula.*" Then, with a smile and a waving of the hands, he or she will mock a *hula-hula* movement.

Most persons from outside Hawaii are only familiar with modern *hula,* what we call the Waikiki or Hollywood *hula* (which bears only passing and campy resemblance to classical *hula*), but even such commercialized dance movements continue to charm and tantalize visitors in the same way real *hula* did in the late 18th Century when dancers "moved their Arms up and down, repeated a Song together, changed their places often, wriggled their backsides and used many lascivious gestures."

That particular description, from Cook's journals, may not sound as formal or spiritual as what Emerson describes above, but in it we see the first exotic swayings of what has since become a Hawaii trademark and "the world's best-known symbol of tropical sensuality." Whether she appears on a souvenir ashtray, or tattoed on a sailor's bicep, or assumes the guise of a cellophane-skirted Betty Grable or Dorothy Lamour in an early Hollywood movie, *the hula girl* always takes stage center here and dominates the Outside World's vision(s) of Hawaii and things Hawaiian.

She's a beautiful anomaly in this day of home computers and mirrored skyscrapers, but she endures, like a dream spirit hovering overhead. You may only see her

Facing page and above: Soft and modern stage lighting bathes the ancient *hula* moves of local dancers during a recent Merrie Monarch Hula Festival held at Hilo on the Big Island.

now and then—perhaps on a floodlit stage in Waikiki or at a local country *luau*—but she's also everywhere—looking up at you from an airline ticket counter, or walking alone down a quiet outer island beach. "Somewhere, behind those Gucci sunglasses," you'll say to yourself, "is a *hula girl.*" Or as Honolulu musician Brother Noland sings it, "she's a coconut girl in a high fashion world."

With such obvious and hidden *hula* girl images in mind, think even bigger and relate to this entire city—Honolulu—as a sprawling, late 20th Century *hula* maiden with flowers in her hair. Those clouds hanging over the mountains are a big puffy *lei,* the green valleys and cliffs are a full *ti* leaf skirt draped around chocolate thighs, and Oahu's many curving beaches are long brown legs standing in the surf. While imagining this, however, remember that beneath that exotic costume is a mischievous and sophisticated island girl who likes to bop till she drops, but who can also, when a sharkskin drum beats or the spirit strikes, sway like a graceful palm and fly like a bird through the movements of a fine *hula.* And while you're trying to psychoanalyze her complex personality, don't forget, as that popular *hapa-haole* song advises, to "keep your eyes on the hands." If you don't, you'll miss many of the fascinating dramas being acted out on Honolulu's every passing street corner...

As an old *hapa-haole* song advises, "Keep your eyes on the hands." The graceful hands and modern *hula* movements on these pages belong to Kanoelehua Kaumeheiwa Miller. Kanoe, a former Miss Hawaii, demonstrated her *hula* artistry during a performance at the Royal Hawaiian Hotel.

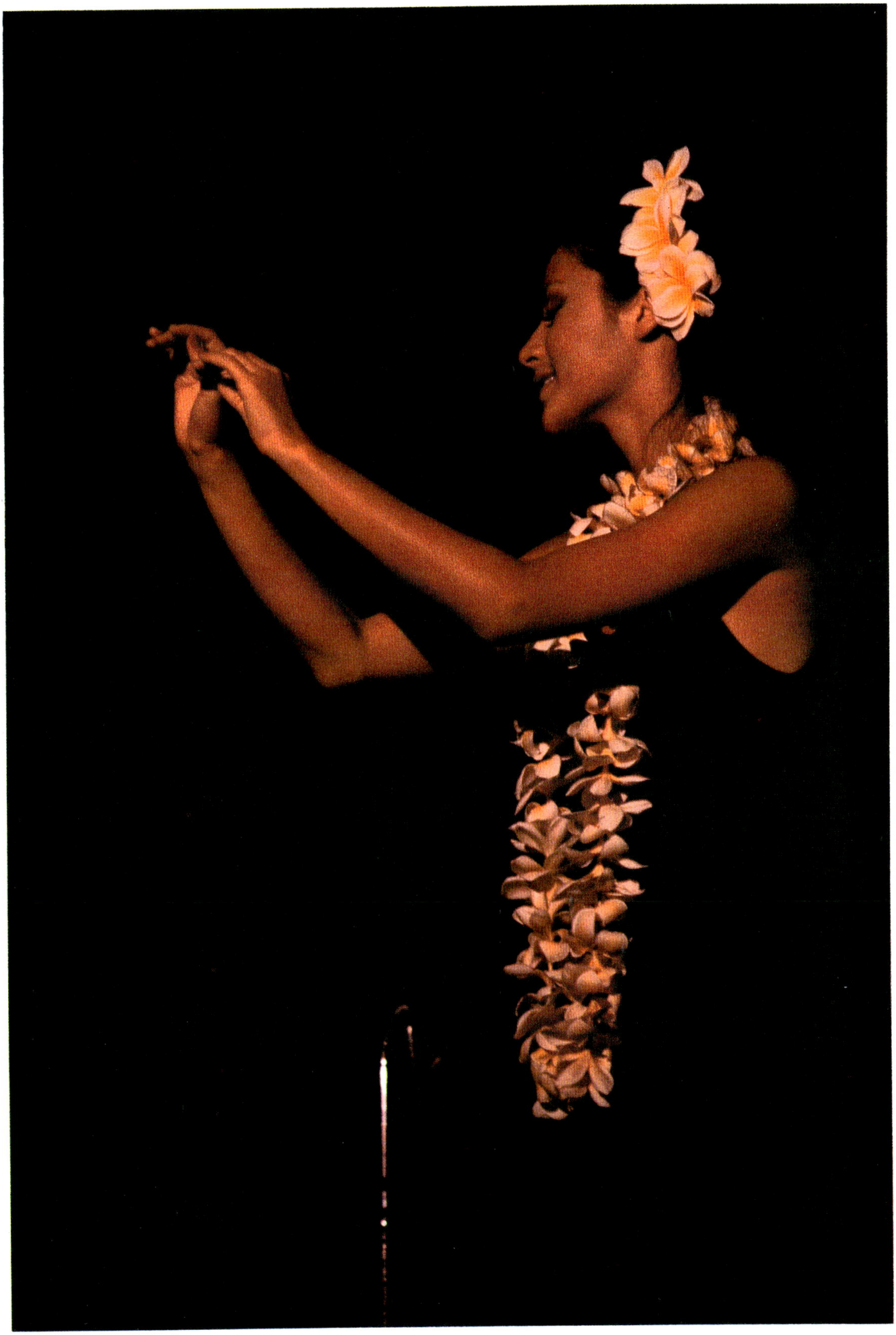

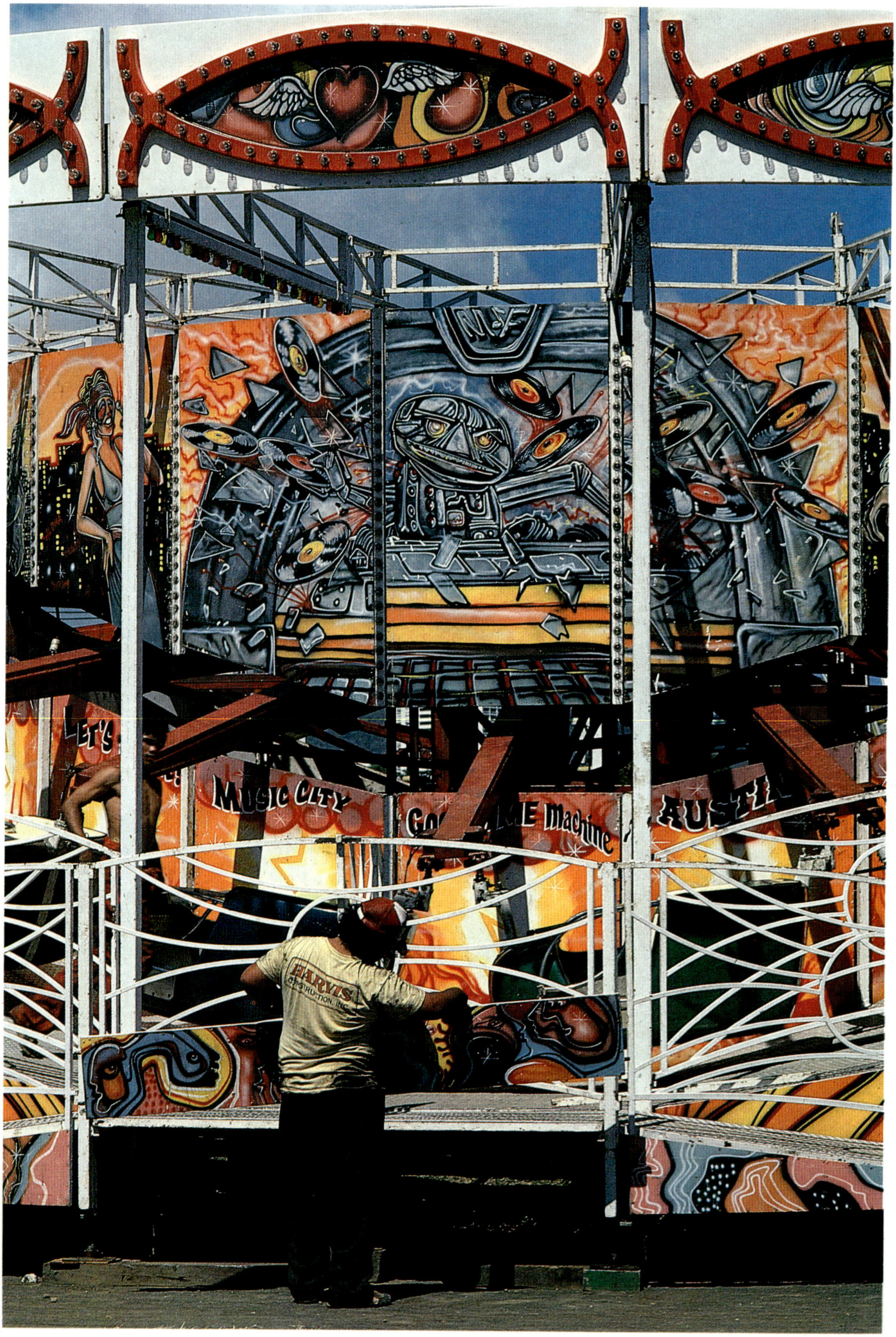
Music City
Machine

One of the first things a newcomer to Hawaii discovers is that the day starts early in Honolulu. Or, to turn the phrase, nights end early. Long before eastern skies are draped with the glow of dawn's peach-pink-grey, Honolulu's only freeway—the Lunalilo H-1—is busy with the hum and bright headlights of Oahu commuters heading toward this city called "town."

Perhaps because they love the bird twitters, fresh flower smells and crystal dew of morning, or maybe because they simply look forward to an early return home, Honolulans tend to be "country types" who like to get to work early, take care of their day's business, then get back home as soon as possible. Because of this early-bird routine, most urban business areas here are virtually abandoned and ghost town-like during evening hours and on weekends. Indeed, you could probably fire a Pershing missile down the middle of Bishop Street at 6 p.m. on any given day and only hit an aging or crippled mynah bird.

During business hours, however, downtown Honolulu (there's no such thing as an "uptown" or "midtown" here) is as chatty, congenial and business-like a civic center as you'll find anywhere. Yes, "business-like," but there's also something ultra-prim, easy-going and personal about this place that distinguishes it from other cities of comparable size.

Facing page and above: Members of the Hawaii Performing Arts Company make themselves up and then live up to their stage roles in a recent HPAC presentation of the Neil Simon musical "Sweet Charity." The HPAC players regularly stride the boards at Oahu's little Manoa Valley Theatre.

"I know we're in the tropics, and I expected the weather to be nicer than it is in other places," commented a recent first-time visitor, "but there's something about this city that is really *different.* The visitor spent an entire day walking around town, shopping at the usual Sears and Woolworth's stores that you find in any American town, but it wasn't until late that evening that the differences he felt suddenly became obvious. He realized, after several hours of wondering and wandering, that (1) "people here don't honk horns" and (2) "there are hardly any signs posted here."

His host laughed and explained that in Honolulu people do not *as a rule* honk car horns (except in an emergency), and that for many years now it has been illegal to erect advertising billboards or oversized flat and neon commercial signs. As a pleasant result, one's mind isn't assaulted by the beep-beep of traffic or the calligraphic and pictorial jangle of painted propaganda you encounter in other urban areas. The only visual distractions, if you want to call them that, are an exotic melange of faces and *local* cultural quirks that make Honolulu marvelous for people-watching. "We're into clean air (the cleanest air in the United States), open green spaces and quiet," the host said proudly. "Amen," said the visitor, and the two repaired to the *lanai* for evening cocktails and *pupus.*

Not that we don't have traffic jams in paradise (we do, and they are a real drag), but even when local folks are lined up bumper-to-bumper in traffic, they rarely, if ever, lean on da horn.

Consider a covey of so-called "sushi girls," all of them members of one or another downtown steno pool, who are giggling animatedly during a lunch break on the *makai-Ewa* lawn at Iolani Palace. While Honolulu's Royal Hawaiian band conducts one of its free Friday afternoon concerts on the palace grounds, these girls are chattering away, sipping at canned passion fruit and guava juices, and poking chopsticks at assorted little rice rolls in takeaway *bento* boxes. It's Aloha Friday, so in keeping with local fashion protocol, these neatly-mascaraed dolly-birds are all wearing brilliantly flowered *muumuus* and *holomuus*. "Naah, naah," they say to one another in pouty pidgin. "How can?" "Oh, da cute."

Nearby, under a royal poinciana tree ablaze in red blossoms, one of the town's leading bankers and a Supreme Court judge (both *kamaaina* chic in reverse-printed aloha shirts) gesture at each other, enjoy brown bag luncheons in the sunshine, and make plans for a late afternoon jog on nearby Ala Moana Beach.

All informal conversation stops, however, when the Royal Hawaiian bandmaster taps his microphone and

Left: The Hawaii Opera Theatre's Joy Simpson as Norma in Vincenzo Bellini's grand romantic tragedy of the same name. *Norma* is set in Gaul. Above: Dancers in another H.O.T. production, Giuseppe Verdi's *La Traviata,* relive the gay life that was Paris in 1870. Both local operatic productions were staged during 1984 at Honolulu's Neal S. Blaisdell Concert Hall.

Hawaii may be farther from any other civilized place than anyplace else, but she boogies right along with the latest in song, dance and other popular fashions. Above: Sonya Mendez and her rock band, Revolución, pump out fine punk sounds at the Wave Waikiki, a very popular "post-modern" nightspot at Waikiki's "edge."
Left and right: The look is surf chic — at Blue Jeans 'n Bikinis and at the new Paradise Express, a one-stop watersports boutique on Keeaumoku Street.

CONVENIENCE

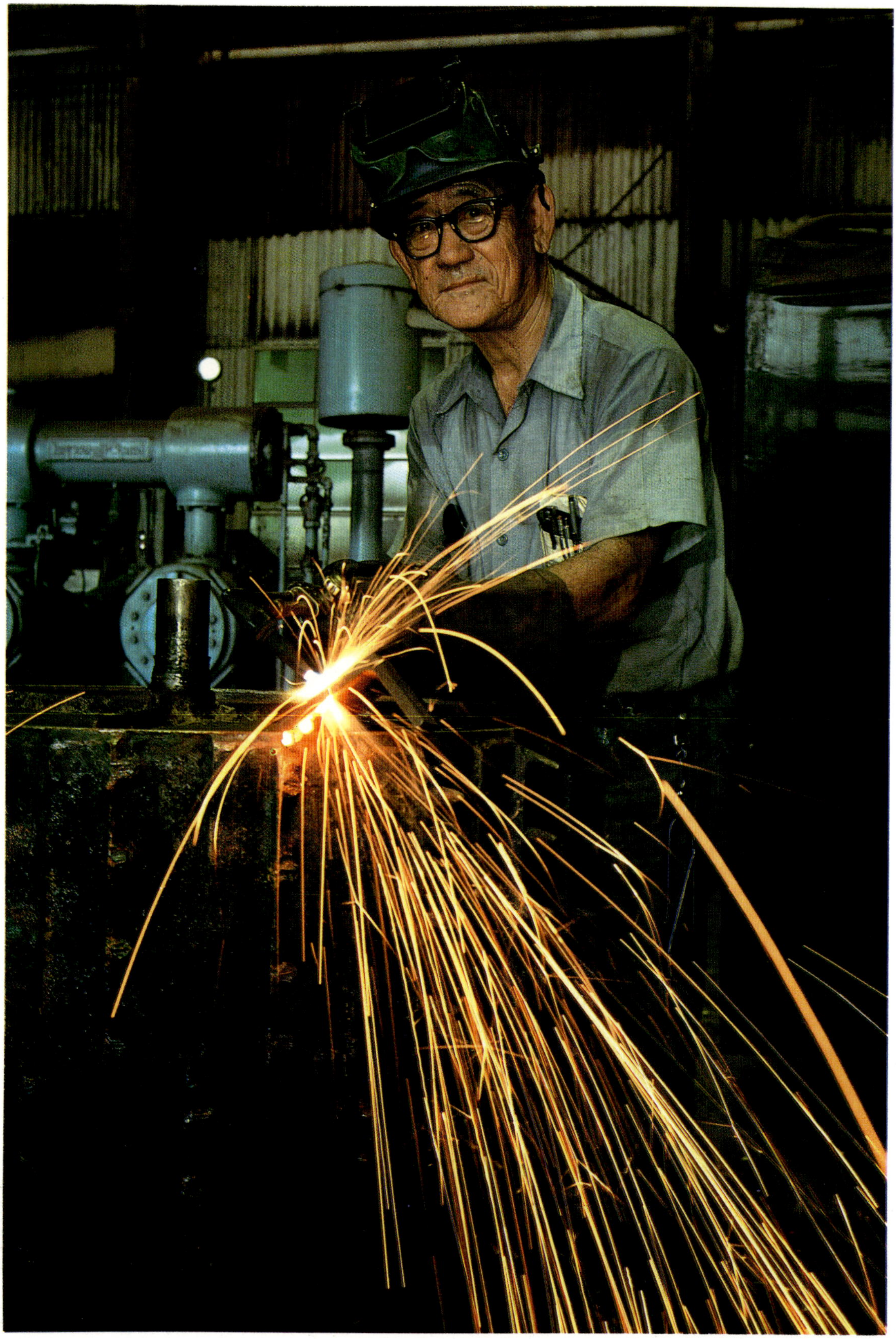

announces that a special guest is about to "dance for us" to the song "Hanalei Moon." The crowd hushes, and as traffic drones down nearby King Street, a tall woman wearing a formal Hawaiian *holoku* and bird-of-paradise blossoms in her hair rolls into a long and lingering *hula* heavy with slow, undulating hip motions. "*Aloha* and *mahalo* plenty," she says later, and the crowd gathered around the bandstand-gazebo ripples with applause.

Stroll *mauka* (toward the mountains) up Bishop Street from Honolulu Harbor, and you'll soon understand why so many sober businessmen who could work bigger fiscal wonders in other industrial centers have chosen to live and trade here. You, too, will be exhilarated by the cooling breeze and hypnotized by the distant emerald green heights framed by the counting houses that line this financial avenue.

"Howzit gang," says a voice on radio station KCCN. "Dis is bruddah Rodney back on the radio. And the following song we would like to dedicate to bruddah Jeff in Nanakuli and Auntie Lani in Papakolea."

The vibrato and tremolo of Hawaiian music fill the air, and it reminds us to remind you to tune into KCCN — 1420 on the AM dial — to hear the sounds of "The World's Only All-Hawaiian Radio Station." Brother Rodney promises he'll be back on the air soon, and as he signs off, a voice says, "*Aloha e na maka-*

Local industry exhibits many faces, as seen, at left, above welding sparks at the old Kekaha Sugar Mill on the island of Kauai, and, above, in the confident eyes of Robert Pfeiffer, the president of the Alexander and Baldwin group of companies. Pfeiffer was photographed in A & B's Matson container yards in Oahu's Sand Island industrial zone.

maka o Ka Leo Hawaii mai ka pua ʻana o ka la i Ha ʻehaʻe a i ka la welowelo i Lehua." "Greetings friends of Ka Leo Hawaii, from where the sun rises at Haʻehaʻe to where the sun streaks across the sky at Lehua."

The speaker is Hawaiian language teacher Larry Lindsey Kimura, and Kimura is beginning an hourly Hawaiian music show he hosts every Sunday night. "This is the only all-Hawaiian language talk show in the world," he says, "so listen close, and remember that for the next hour (from 7 to 8 p.m.) we'll be speaking *only* in Hawaiian."

Calls begin coming in—from Oahu and the Outer Islands—and the subjects discussed cover everything from family problems to esoteric Hawaiian culture. Very few people still speak the nearly extinct Hawaiian language, so Kimura's show is a rare and poignant reminder of days when everybody here did.

Move on down the dial, and you'll hear things like the latest Town & Country surf report ("Sorry, bruddahs, but today we get notʻing. Queens, Kaisers and Ala Moana are all flat like one pancake."), or "The Rainbow Warrior Football Network," where a burly Irishman, Jim Leahey, otherwise known as Kimo Leahi, is saying "ʻnuff already" as the University of Hawaii Rainbows lose another spirited game.

"It's these little local things that hooked me on this

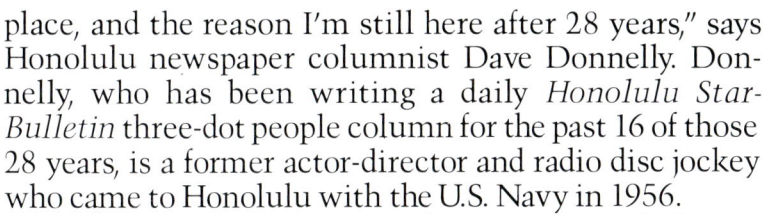

place, and the reason I'm still here after 28 years," says Honolulu newspaper columnist Dave Donnelly. Donnelly, who has been writing a daily *Honolulu Star-Bulletin* three-dot people column for the past 16 of those 28 years, is a former actor-director and radio disc jockey who came to Honolulu with the U.S. Navy in 1956.

"I left once, in August of '58, to attend theatre classes at the University of Iowa, but I was back in ten months. It was quite a decision for me, because at Iowa I was surrounded by some of the finest writers and theatre people in the world, but it *wasn't* Hawaii. I guess I was too used to the laid back attitude, and warmth of weather and people, and after only one winter of digging my car out of snowbanks, I had to come back."

Donnelly says he's constantly amazed by the preconceptions and distorted images most non-Hawaii people have about Hawaii. "This is probably because most people think of Waikiki and tourism when they think of Hawaii, but it's also because many people think that those of us who live here are all nice little island boys and girls who don't know what's going on in the rest of the world. The truth of the matter is that we really do know what's going on over there — and that's why we're here."

As an example of such Mainland condescension, he recalls a visit he made to New York to inquire into se-

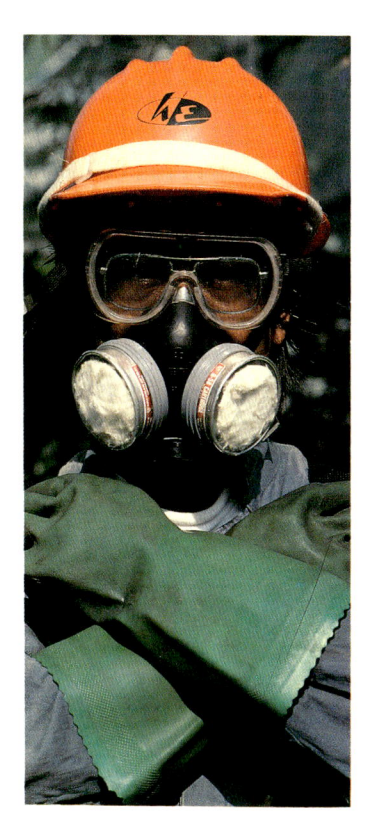

Left: One of the first things Hawaii visitors see on their way from Honolulu Airport to their Waikiki hotel is a giant Dole pineapple that performs double-duty as a water tank. Above: An employee of the Oahu-based Hawaiian Electric company pauses for a portrait.

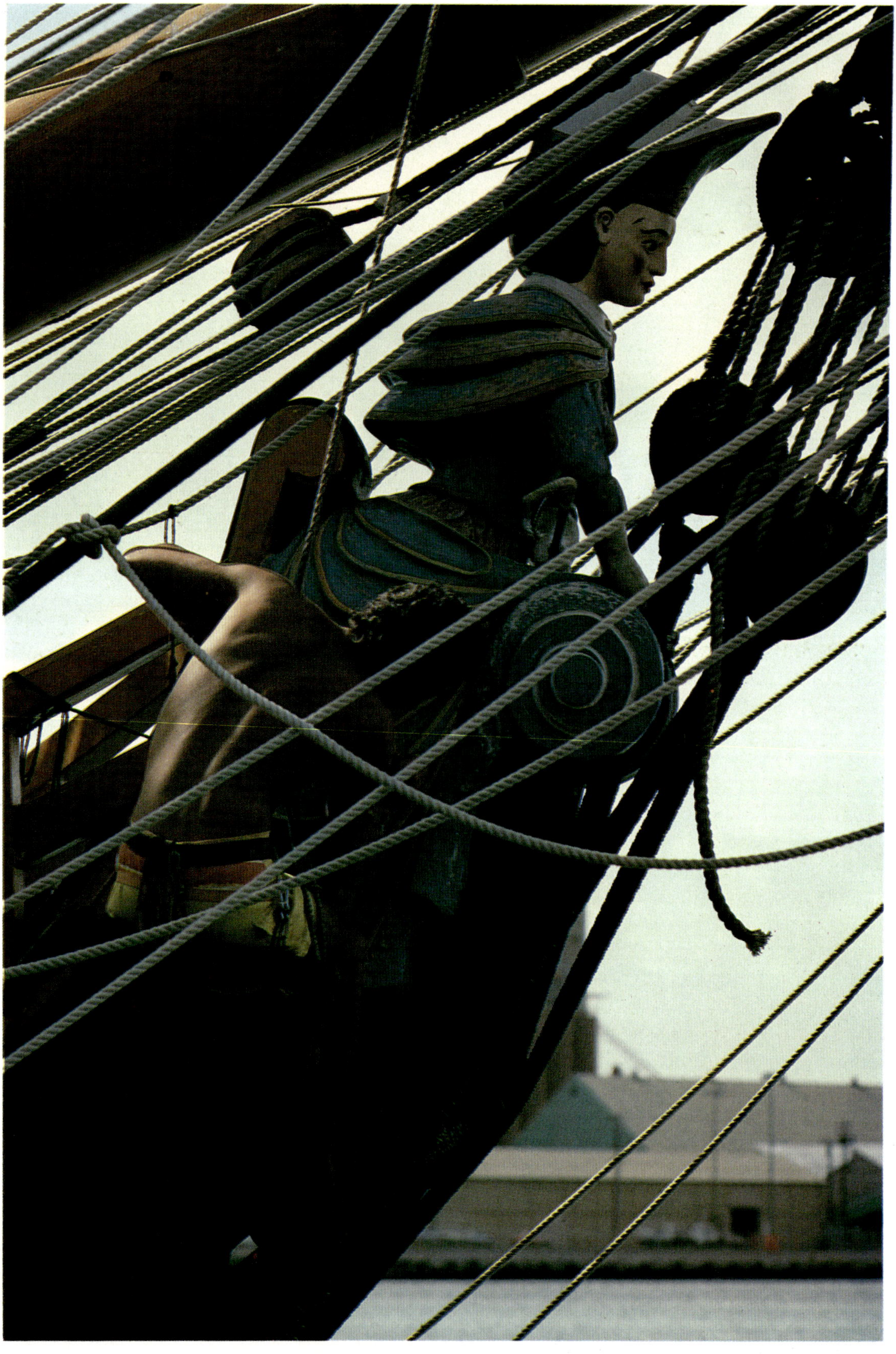

curing the rights to stage a Honolulu production of the play "Who's Afraid of Virginia Woolf." "Here I am in this big sophisticated office in Manhattan, inquiring after the rights to 'Virginia Woolf,' and the nicely dressed secretary in this plush office says to me, 'Will you be doing the play in English?' I nearly fell out of my chair when she said that. And *they* think that we're provincial? That we're out of touch?"

To chide such people, Donnelly's column regularly identifies recipients of a dubious Statehood Recognition Award. These awards go to Mainland Americans and others who refer to Hawaii as a "foreign" country or do silly things such as send a package from Boston to Honolulu with a customs declaration form attached. A favorite recent incident deserving of a Donnelly Statehood Recognition Award involved a local man who called an Amtrak National Railways office on the Mainland to make a train booking. After he explained his needs and told the Amtrak reservationist that he was from Hawaii, she politely informed him that "sorry, but we don't take reservations from outside the United States." After Donnelly published an item about that incident, an Amtrak official called to advise him that Amtrak's computer would soon be updated to include Hawaii — the 50th State — in its roster of eligible and recognized United States.

Facing page and above: Crew members on board a perfect replica of the famous Bounty *sailing ship take advantage of a recent Honolulu stopover to touch up their handsome lady of the high and mighty seas.*

Facing page and above: These mariners, who pursue different lifestyles on different kinds of watercraft, all call Oahu's Kewalo boat basin home. All were photographed on the same sunny Honolulu day.

I mean, yes, it's true, we don't have subways and smog (except, of course, when a volcano erupts, but we call that "vog"), and none of our buildings are more than 45 stories high, but we're not that far away and out of touch. The average Honoluluan may talk and dress funny, but he does speak English, and he more likely than not has a television set on which he watches the same daily network news broadcasts being watched in Philadelphia, Atlanta and San Diego.

Are you interested in art? Then wander through our Civic Center area, where you'll find—inside a two block zone—important works by Henry Moore, Isamu Noguchi, Marisol Escobar and Jean Charlot gracing private and public buildings and open spaces. Music and dance? Well, besides a full-fledged symphony and opera and ballet companies, we're into punk, jazz, rock and roll, *and* nearly anything that's hip and popular in Japan, China, Korea and the Philippines. Not to mention the highest concentration of Hawaiian musicians and *hula* dancers in the world.

"Plus," says Donnelly, "we've got more airplanes flying in and out of this place than nearly any other place in the world, so if you aren't seeing enough Kabuki, you can go to Japan in seven hours, or, if you need more theatre and music than you're getting here, you can fly to Los Angeles or San Francisco in four-and-a-

PARADISE COVE

On following pages: Each of these three local fishermen had a different fish story to tell — one about a golden *mahimahi* (page 95), and the others about a silvery *ahi* and a scale-tipping marlin.

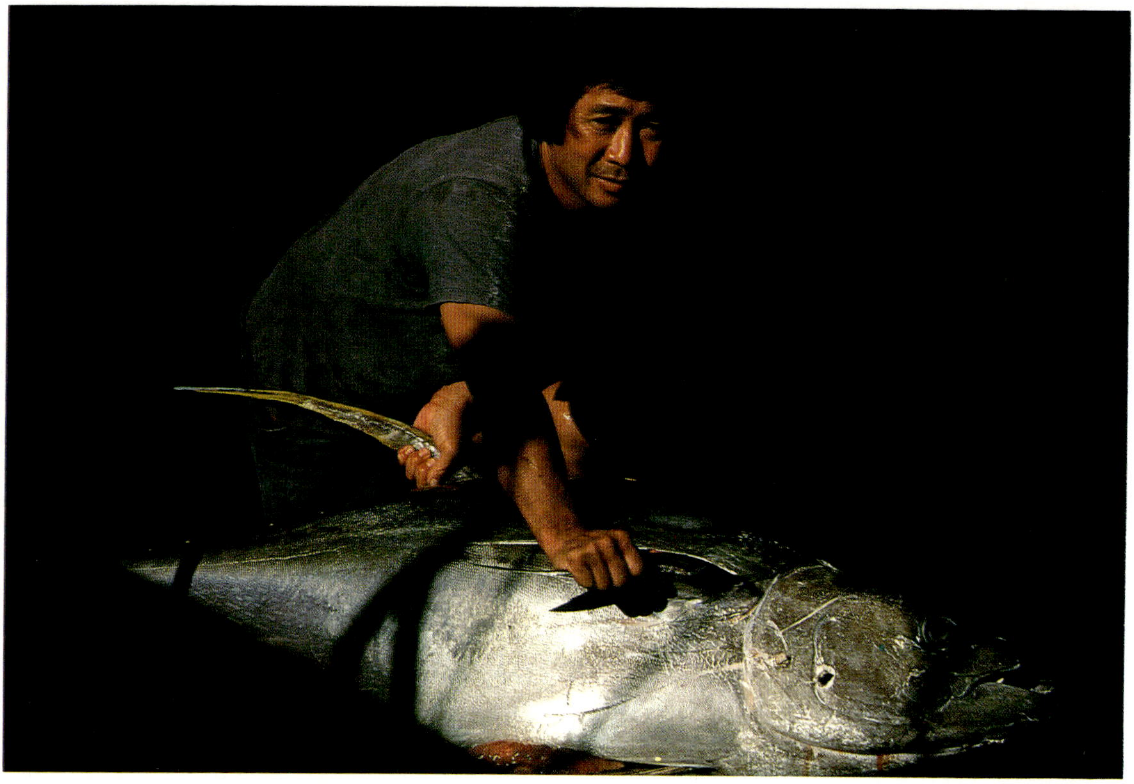

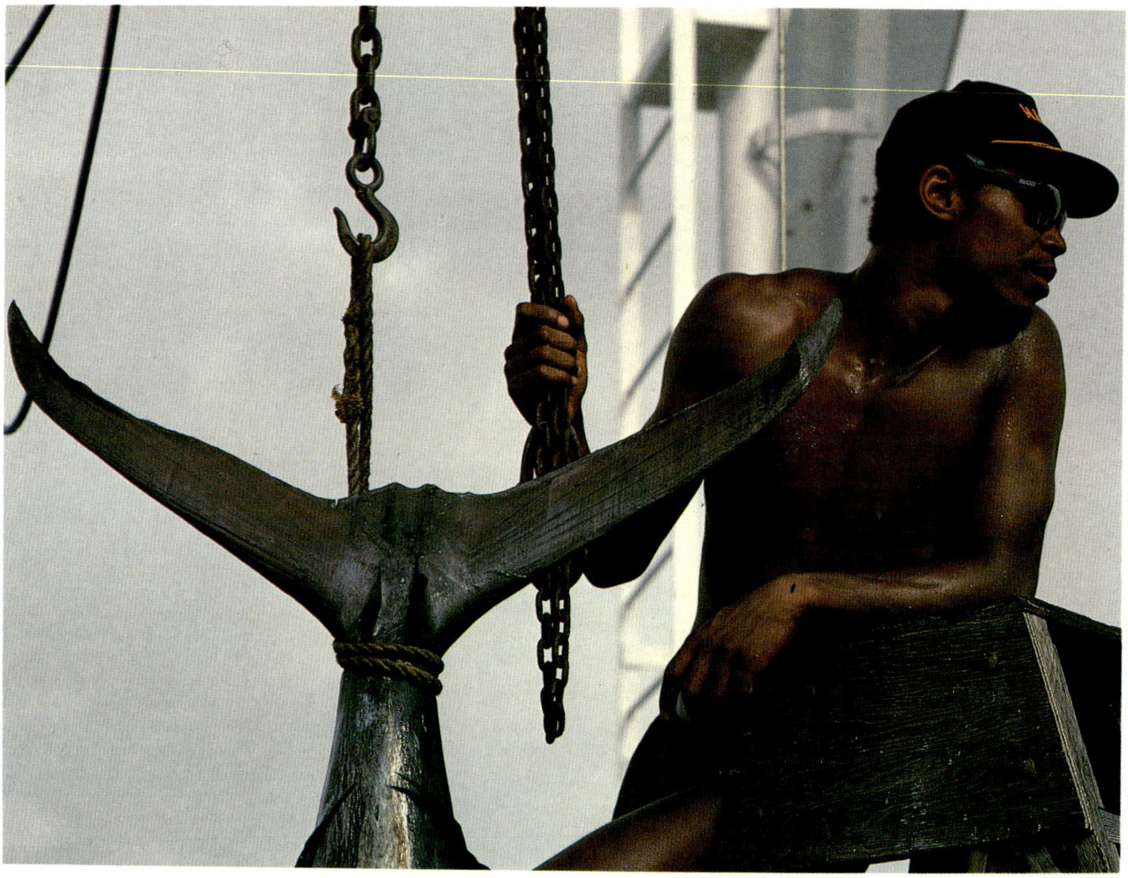

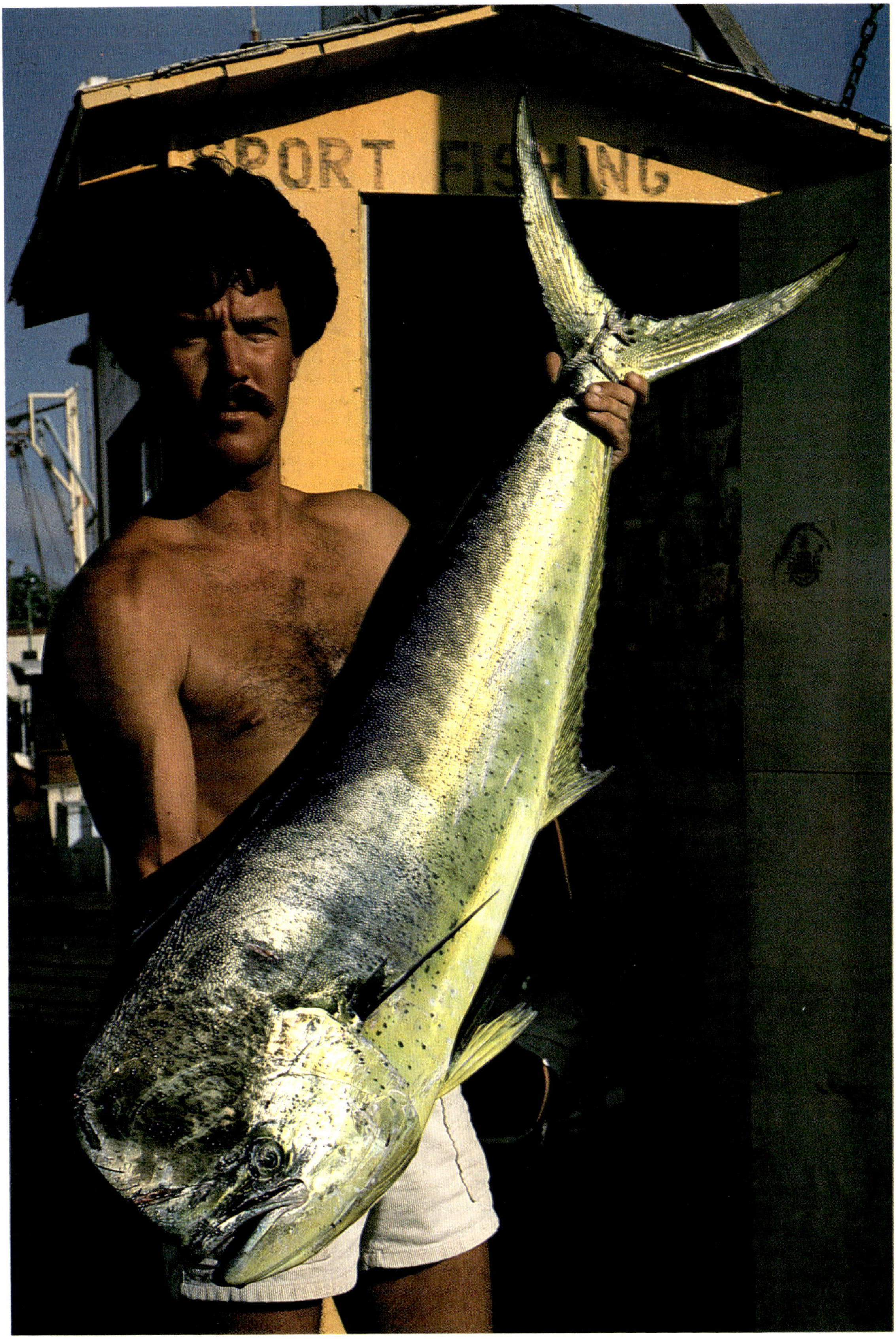
SPORT FISHING

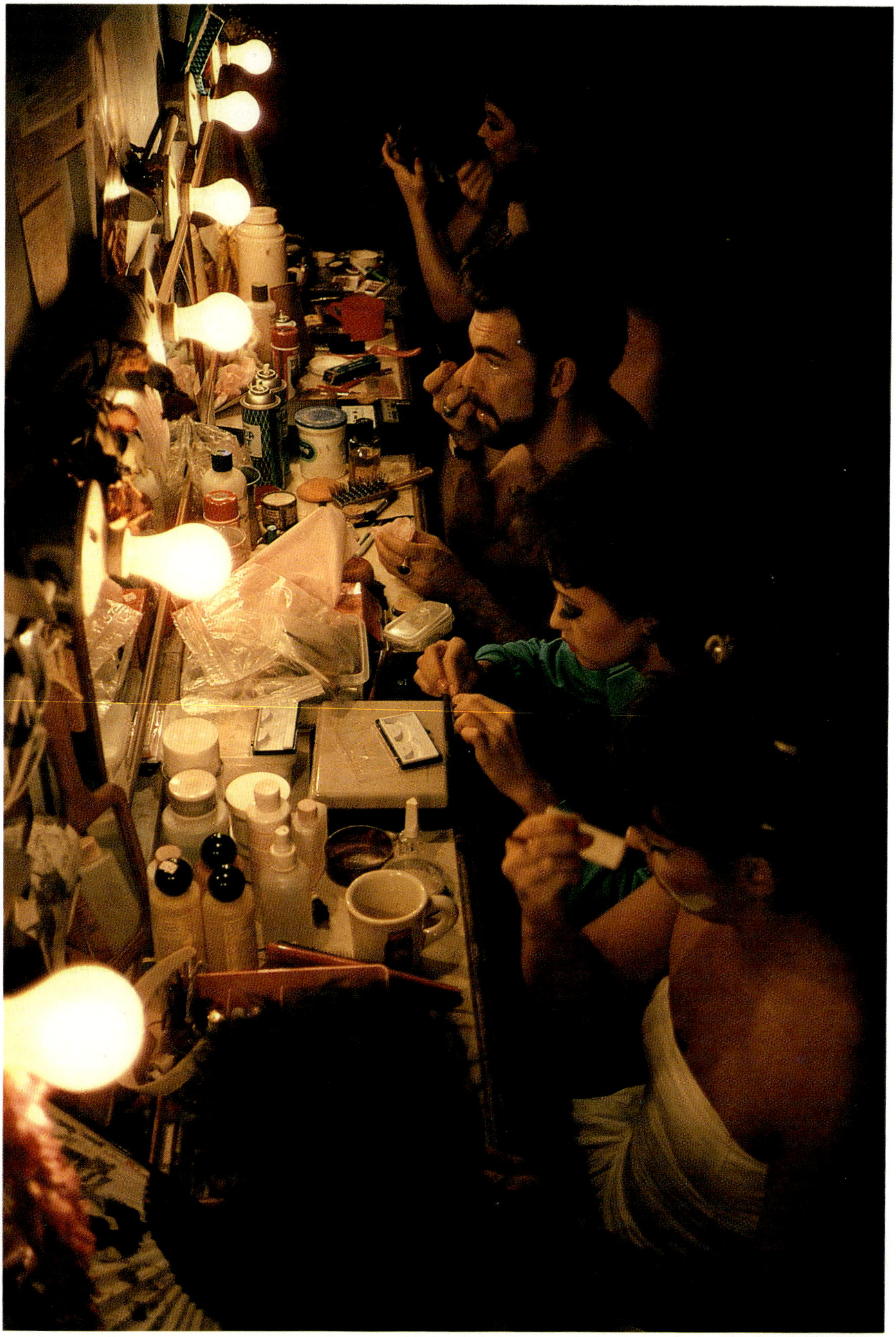

half hours and get your fill of the finest actors and musicians in the world."

After living in Honolulu for say two or three years, you become used to her abundant ethnic distinctions, distractions and what visiting author Didion calls her hidden "eccentricity."

One of those eccentric points is a typical, All-American supermarket, where bemused visitors are always surprised to find "local foods" such as *daikon,* Chinese crack seeds, fresh *laulaus* and dried beef *pipikaula* stocked as "regular" sales items. What newcomer wouldn't smile after hearing a computer-originated voice at Foodland Supermarket call out: "One half pound of *gobo,* fifty-nine cents ... One pound of *poi,* one dollar-fifty cents ... one package of *nori,* eighty-nine cents ... two pounds of *opakapaka,* twelve dollars ... one half pound of *alae* salt, sixty-nine cents ... one *lilikoi* chiffon cake ..." and so on, "bleep-bleep" and "thank you." Now if they could only program that Mainland *haole* voice to speak in local pidgin dialects.

Don't forget to pay a visit to Honolulu's so-called "Chinatown." There, within a hundred yard radius of the old Wo Fat Chinese restaurant, you'll find an Itaewon-style Korean rock and roll club, a Japanese all-night donut shop, a Filipino dance hall with a live *mambo* band, three Vietnamese cafes, and a raucous

The E. K. Fernandez Carnival is in town and "Ladies and gentlemen, it will soon be showtime." Two local carnival gypsies, facing page and above, put the finishing touches on two of E. K.'s carnival midway rides.

Hawaiian music night club that caters to hormonious boys who prefer being girls.

Even Honolulu's most minor of minorities, the blacks, enjoy a Chinatown scene all their own: Their turf is Smith Street, where local *popolos,* as blacks are called here, can be seen hanging out and high-fiving one another at the Wonder Bar—or having their hair processed at the Vogue hair-styling Salon. There used to be a proper soul food cafe on Smith Street, but word has it that the proprietor lost too much business to the Japanese donut shop and was forced to close.

Chinatown. The name evokes images of *cheong-sam* girls, Charlie Chan and dragon dances. You'll find all of those things and more in Honolulu's Chinatown, but in recent years it has been quickly losing its Chineseness and has evolved into more of a "Mix-Mix Town." Next door to a venerable Chinese society's *mahjong* hall, you'll now more likely find a fancy design studio instead of a noodle shop full of clacking chopsticks.

Such social and ethnic distinctions and mixings soon become a part of your daily routine and melt one into the other like a big "local" blur. You learn to grunt in appropriate pidgin phrases when dealing with a gas station attendant or security guard. And you take for granted the fact that *everybody* takes their shoes off before walking into a local home. If a person doesn't take off his shoes, the lady of the house looks at him as if he's some kind of extraterrestrial who doesn't know any better.

Some people move here, live for a while, and soon find themselves in the grip of what is popularly called "Rock Fever." This psychosomatic affliction is a form of open air claustrophobia, and it usually strikes folks who are used to "wide open spaces" where "y'all ken drive a hunnert miles in a flat-out bee line."

Unfortunately, there's not much one can do for these people, except maybe ship 'em back to Cheyenne or Albuquerque. For one thing, there isn't much of that kind of open space, save in a few ranch zones of the Big Island. And second, all of these islands are very intimate places — like mountain top villages or big cruise ships — where you either get into the local swing of things or condemn yourself to life in a stuffy mental funk.

Those of us who love living here have learned to cope with the close quarters of the place by unconsciously imposing a sort of finely-tuned sense of time and space warp on our activities. Instead of being obsessed with vast land spaces, we open up to the sea and sky. And when we do indulge in land travel, we simply dial down our expectations. We don't *expect* to travel far, so instead of flooring the gas pedal, we slow down and really *get into* the amount of space we do travel through to compensate for the lack of distances involved.

The old Club Hubba Hubba, left, is a reminder of Honolulu's busy World War II partying days on downtown's Hotel Street. And Tin Tin Chop Suey, above, has long been a favorite late night noodles spot frequented by downtowners in the know.

What happens, inevitably, is that people who settle down here tend to become very self-satisfied and happy in their particular valley filled with cooling mists and rainbows. That's why you'll often meet island people who rarely ever travel outside a five to ten mile area that includes their home, office and children's school.

"Why leave clean air and blue skies here for smog and grey skies over there," explained an elderly man when he was asked why he had never left the islands. His excuse sounds like an unsophisticated thing to say, but even the most jaded traveler finds himself saying things like that after a few years of living in Hawaii.

A good case in point involves a *haole* sports writer who moved to Hawaii many years ago, went to work for a local newspaper, and shortly thereafter fell in love with and married a local Japanese woman. After a few years of living, loving and working here, he took his local bride for a long-planned vacation to his hometown on the West Coast. He was supposed to be gone for three weeks, but instead cut his trip short and returned a week early.

"What are you doing back here so soon?" his surprised friends asked.

"Well, if you want to know the truth," he said, "I was bored to death. I tried to have a good time, and everybody was real nice and all, but, well, there were just too many *haoles* over there — and I didn't feel *at home.*"

When the sun goes down, and most of Honolulu has gone home, downtown's colorful Chinatown area comes alive. Above: "Acts of Love" on Hotel Street. Right: A decidedly local lady models the latest in New Wave fashions on nearby Maunakea Street.

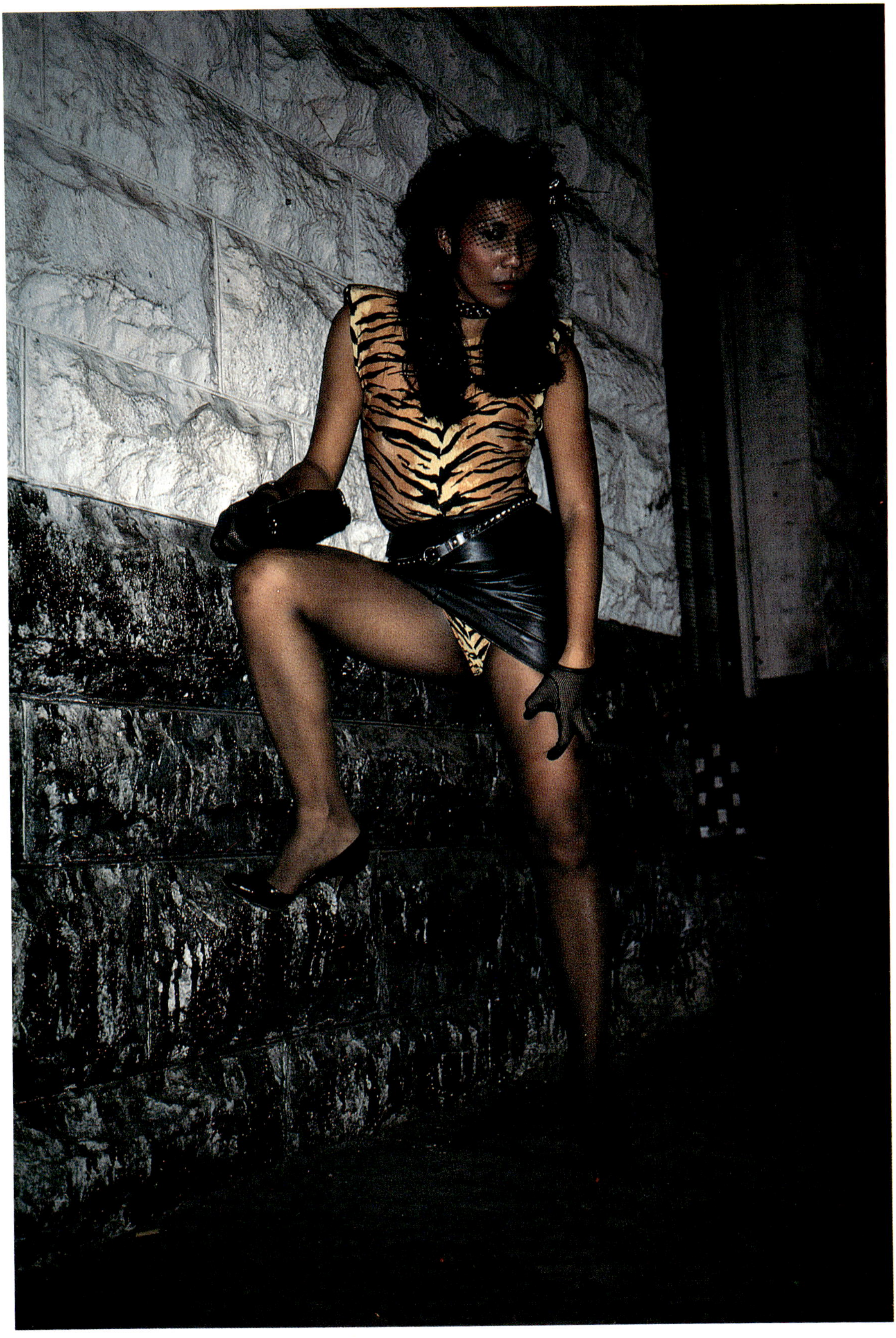

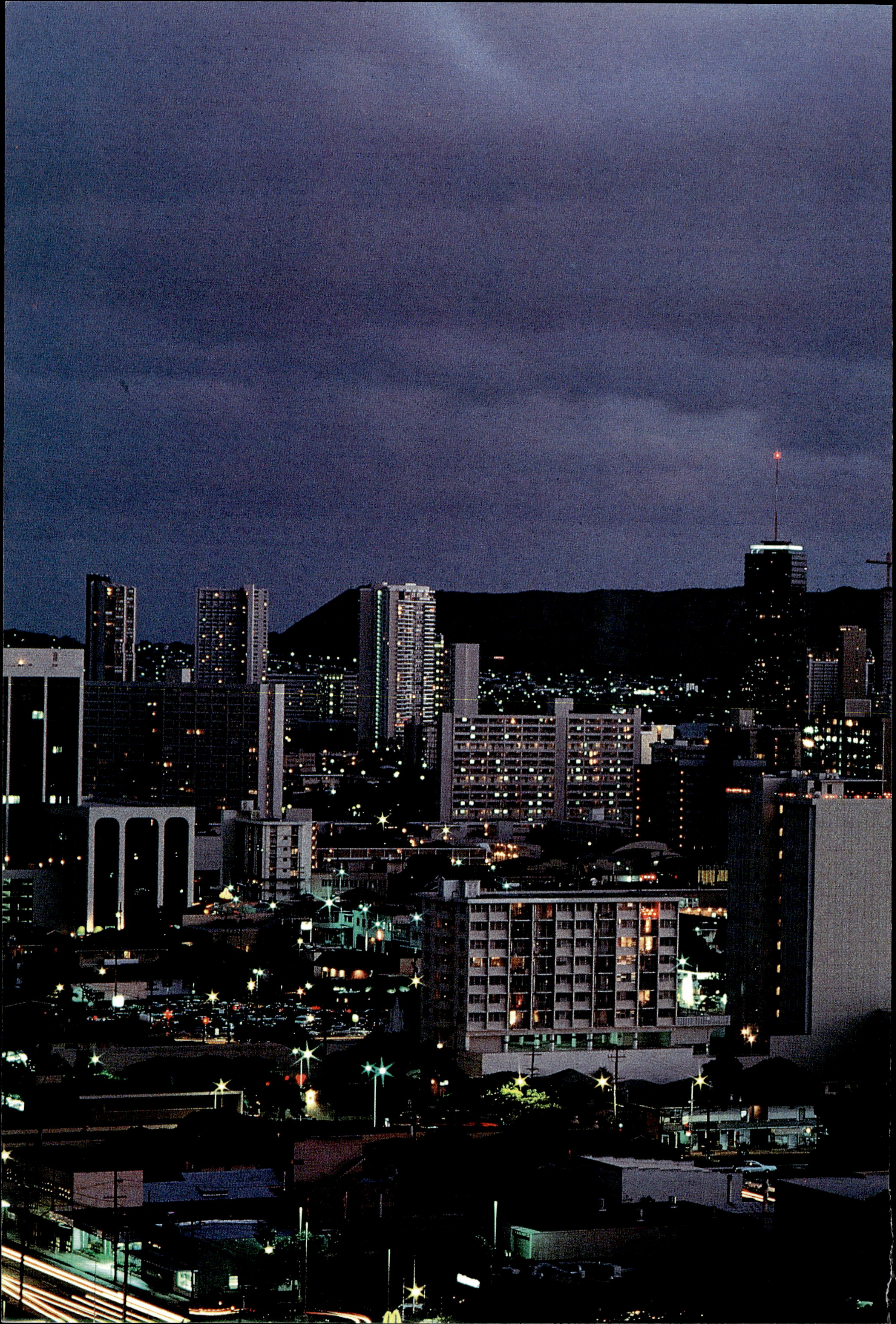

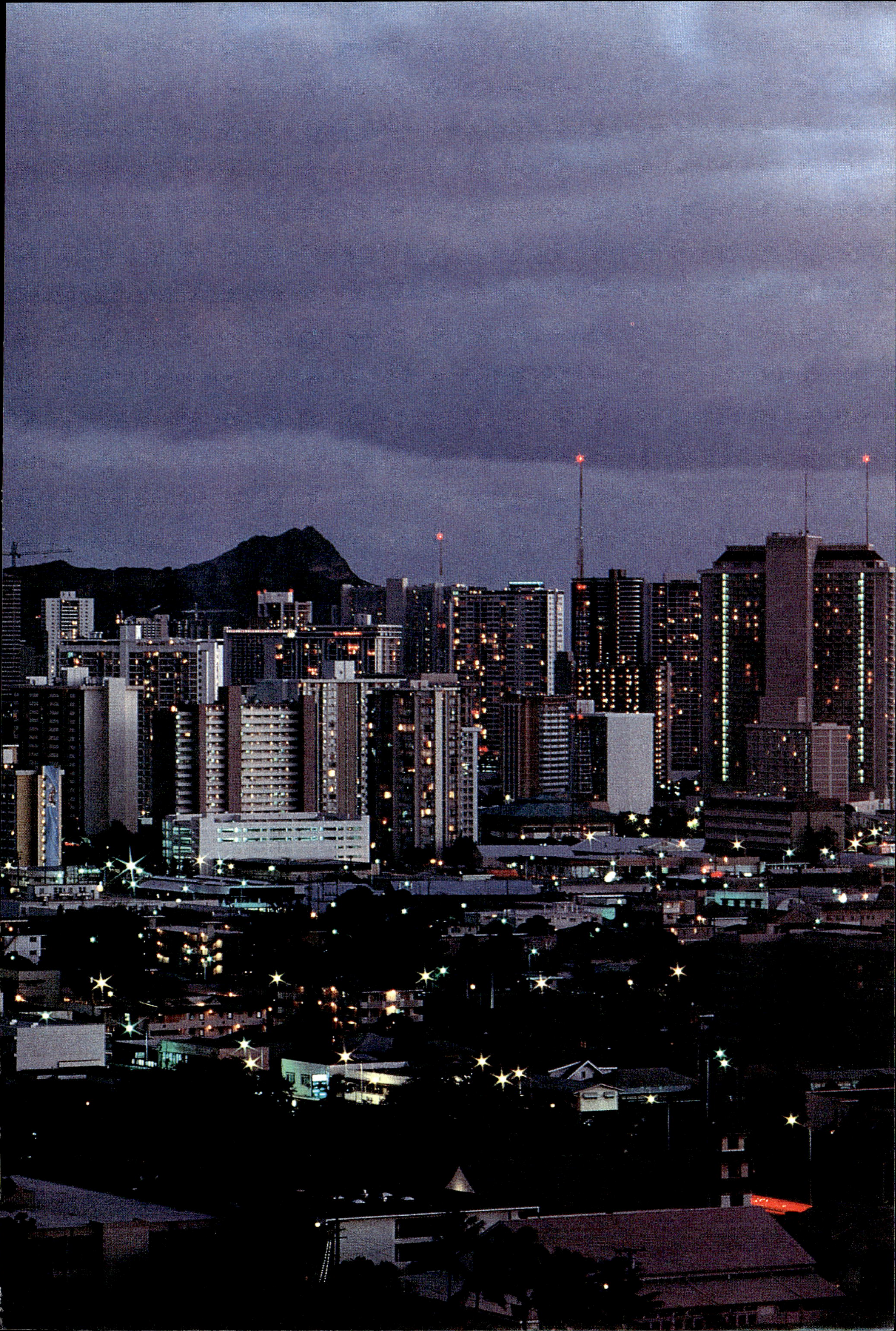

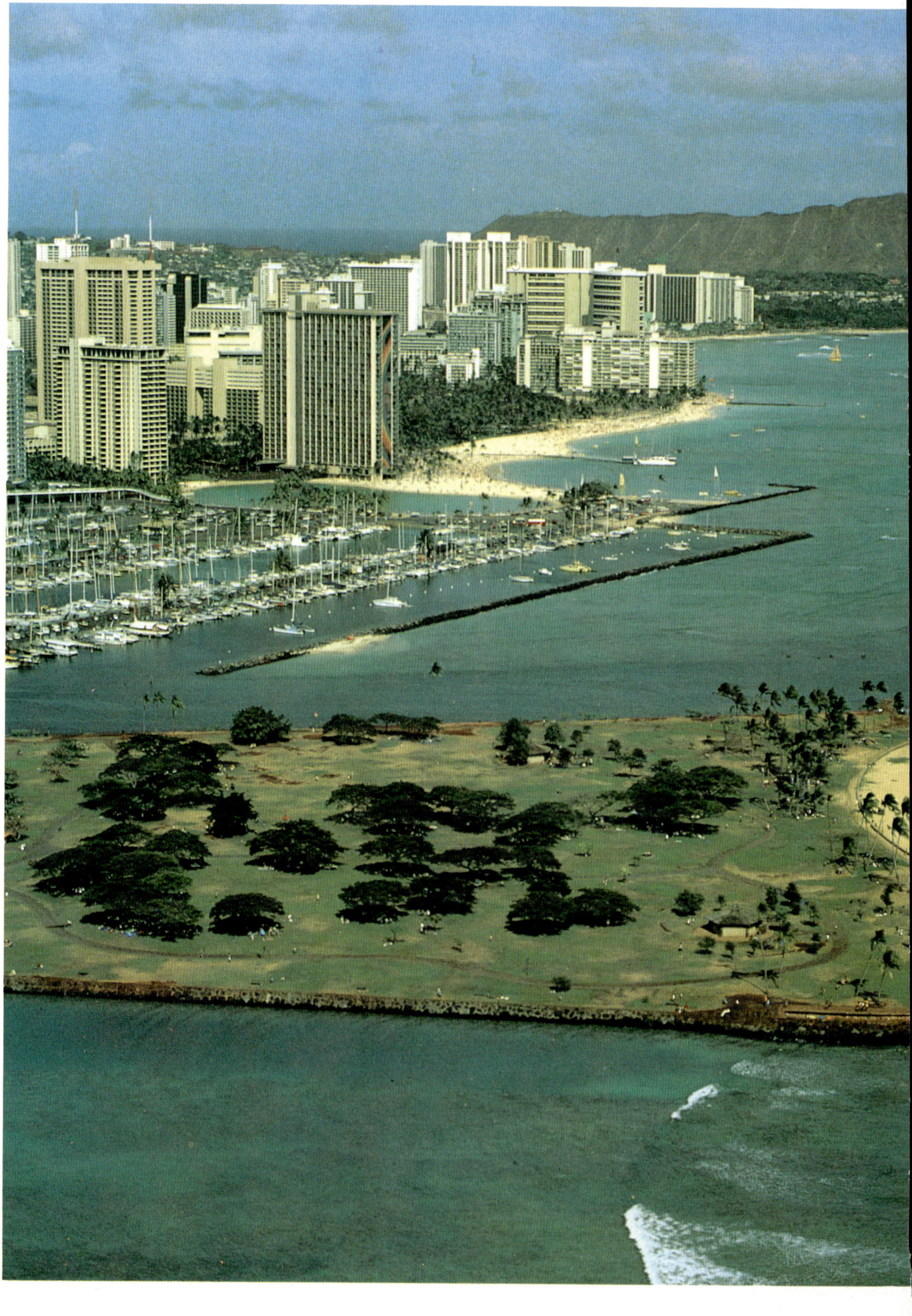

On preceding pages: Waikiki and Diamond Head crater glow like neon jewels in a Honolulu twilight.
Left: A helicopter view of Magic Island, the Ala Wai yacht basin and Waikiki, "the most famous beach in the world."
Above: Shirley Rogers, a noted surf photographer, entertains the other side of a camera lens.

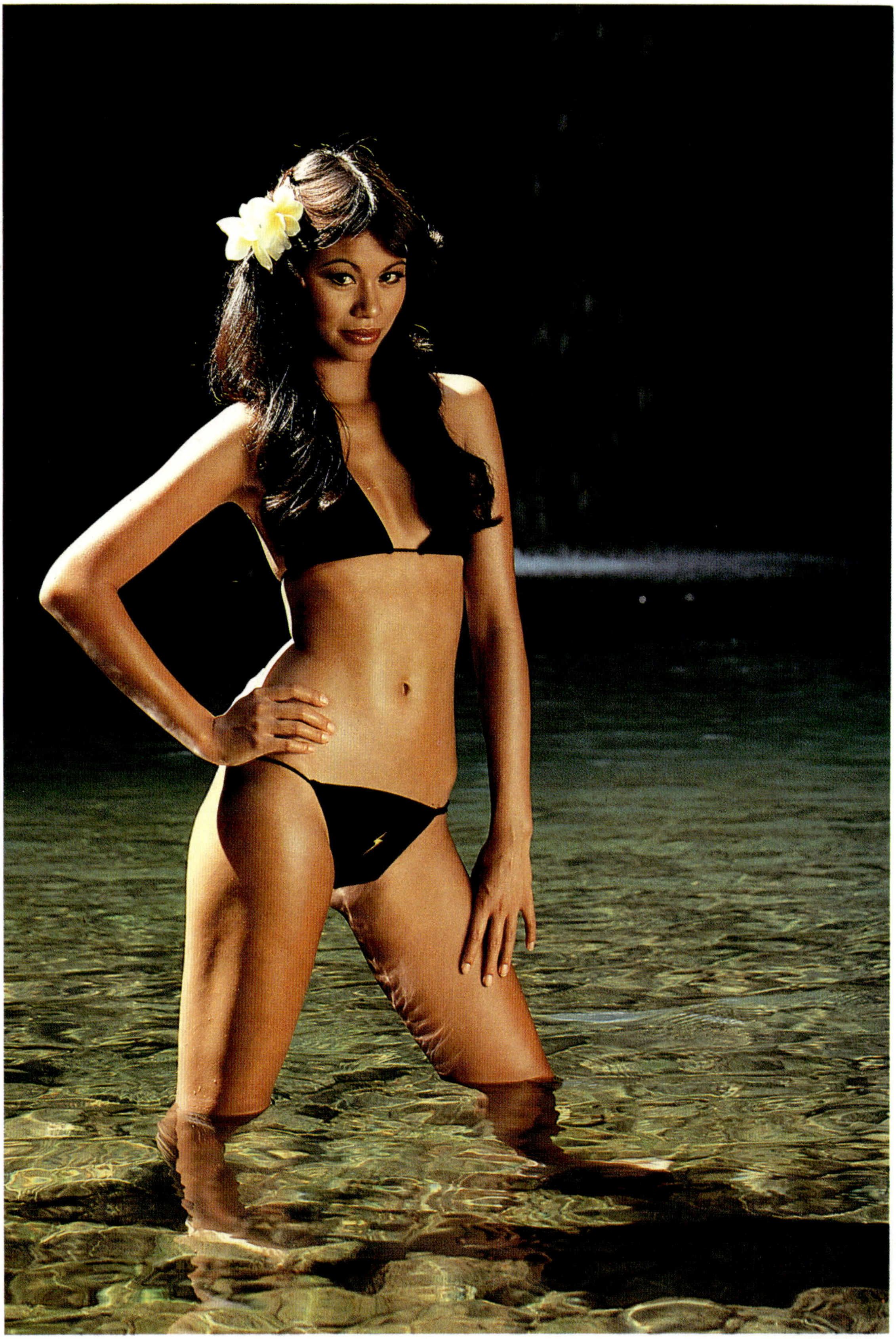

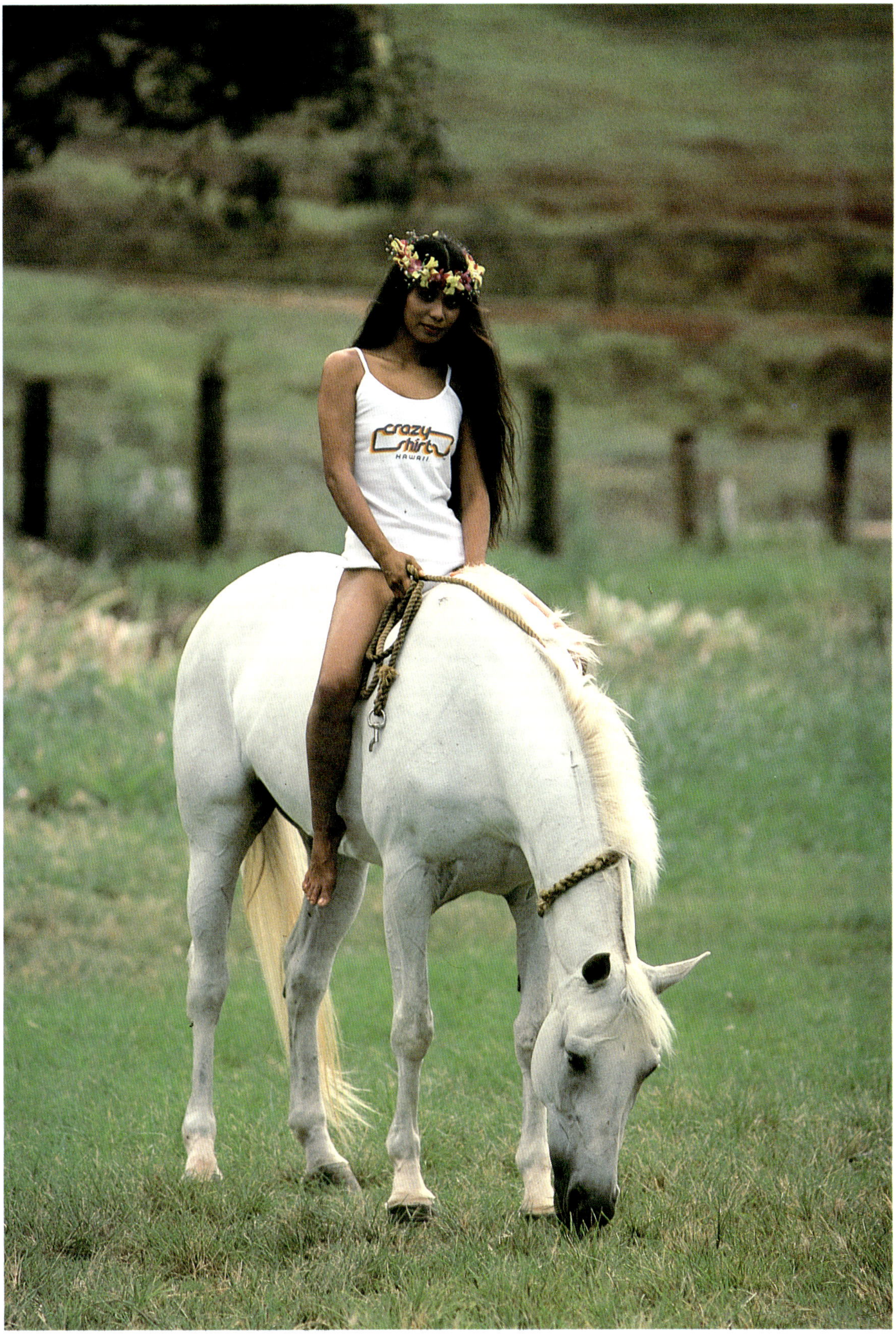
crazy
shirt
HAWAII

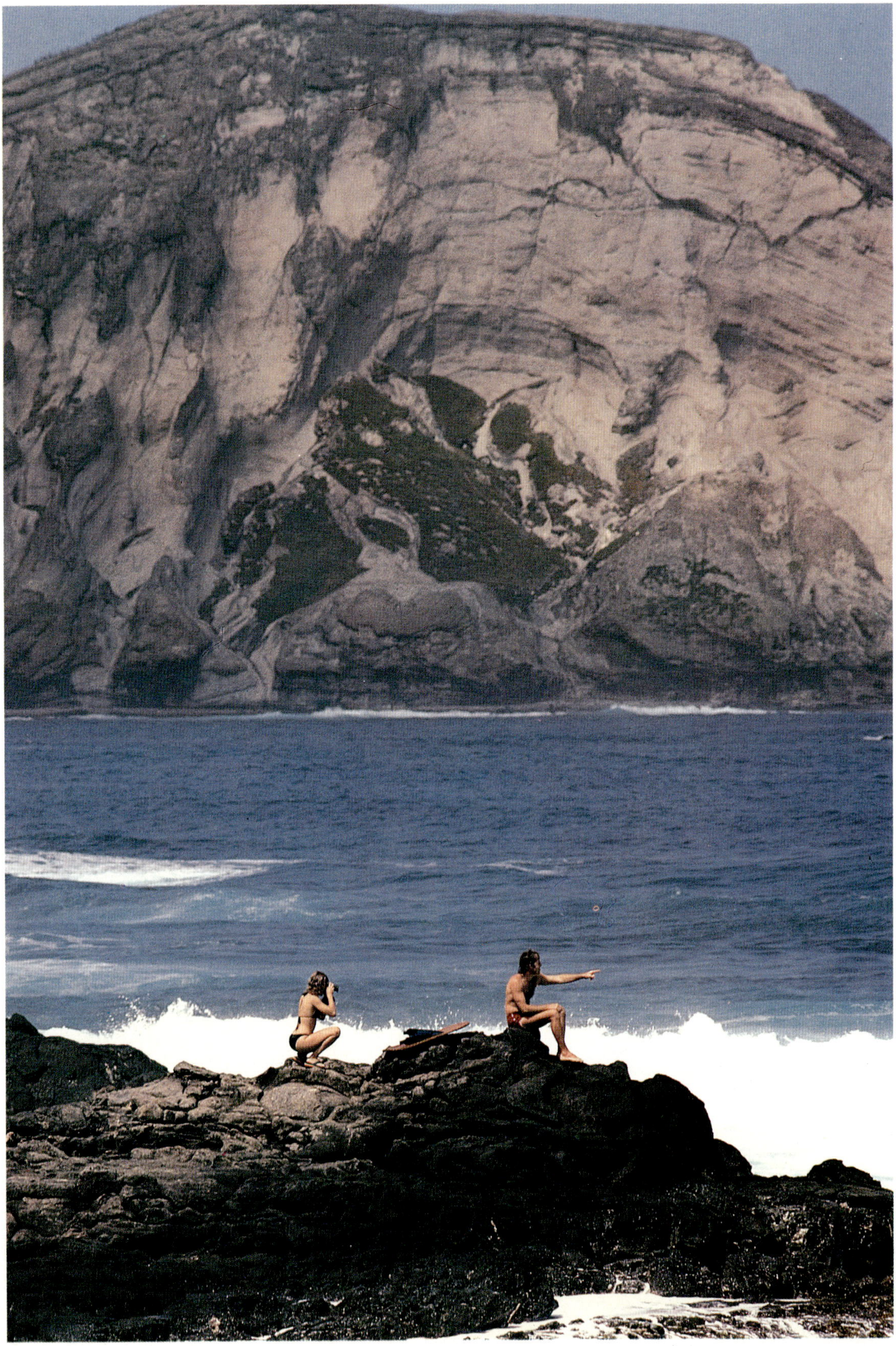

It is unquestionably in Polynesia that the great oceanic pull is felt most strongly, away from continents, from civilization, toward ease, voluptuousness and warm beauty of place and people...

—Author Gavan Daws, in
A Dream of Islands, 1980.

If you must resist, and still don't want to believe this is Paradise, then we suggest that you commission a Paradise Pedicab to take you to the 1000 to 1200 blocks of Beretania Street where you can amuse yourself at Paradise Amusement and browse through Paradise Antique Arts before having your hair cut at the Paradise Barber Shop. Or better yet, play pool at Paradise Cue in the Kapiolani district before having a sauna at the Paradise Health Spa in Kapahulu.

Not paradisiacal enough? Then how about having your shirts pressed at the Paradise Laundry? Or a stroll through Paradise Park? Or a few minutes of heavenly meditation at the Paradise Chapel? You can even, Paradise-seekers, improve on all the above visions by first buying a pair of rose-colored glasses at the Paradise Optical Company on Bishop Street.

It never ends, this local paradise stuff. Look through the Honolulu telephone directory and you'll find more than fifty separate listings for Paradise this and Paradise that. There's even a Paradise Da Kine (*da kine* being an indeterminate identifier for *whatevah*). Bored by all the Paradise available on Oahu? Then *hele on* to the Big Island where you can drive a Paradise Used Car and book a Paradise Safari. Or fly to Maui where you can rent movie tapes from Paradise Video and hock your belongings at the Paradise Pawn Shop.

We're beginning to sound silly, but after all, why did Hollywood filmmakers choose *Blue Hawaii* as the place to shoot all the outdoor scenes in movies such as *Bali Hai, South Pacific, King Kong* and *Fantasy Island*? Remember Burt Lancaster and Deborah Kerr rolling around in Hawaii's sand and surf in 1953's *From Here to Eternity*? Or even better, how about delicious Dolores Del Rio performing a sizzling "mating dance" in *Bird of Paradise* (1932) filmed on the Kona Coast?

These pictures of Paradise may sometimes seem slightly out of focus (given encroaching urbanization, isolated incidents of violent crime and Hawaii's high cost of living), but as that popular song notes, this really is "almost Paradise, how could we ask for more?"

There's something rather intoxicating about Ha-

Facing page: While a vacationing he is photographed by a bikinied she, Paradise — in the happy guise of a seaside lava flow, blue seas and Rabbit Island in the background — provides the backdrop and a dramatic view of Makapuu Beach on Oahu's idyllic Windward Side.
Above: A smiling local boy sticks not his head, but his body, into the sand at Oahu's nearby Kailua Beach.

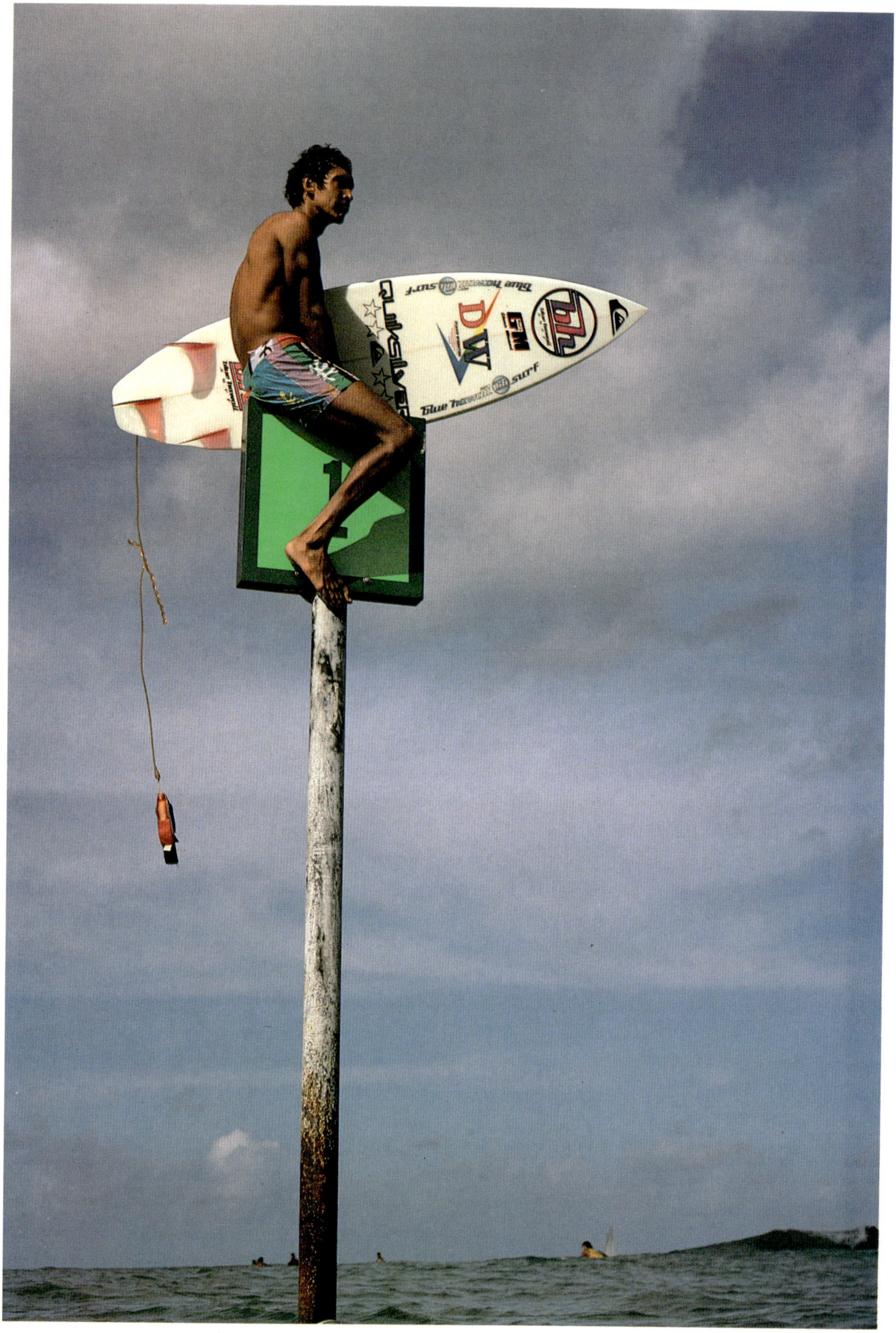

waii's soft and cooling tradewinds, green mountains, aquamarine waters and fawn beaches, and such physical euphoria lends itself to Paradise-calling. And it's not a new and strictly commercial phenomenon, because even old time Hawaiians were fond of using the word *lani,* for heavenly or heaven (also spelled *'iu lani*), to describe local people, places and things.

Flip through a copy of the important book *Place Names of Hawaii* (by Mary Kawena Pukui, Samuel H. Elbert and Esther T. Mookini), and you'll find dozens of such "heavenly" names. Above Kaimuki on Oahu rises Maunalani, the "heavenly mountain"; on Maui there's pretty Pukalani (originally spelled Pu'ukalani), "the hill of the heavens"; and on nearly every island you'll find a place called Kapiolani, which refers to that wondrous "arch of heaven" called a rainbow. Many of these place names are adopted as girls' names. The most beloved princess in Hawaiian history, for example, was the beautiful Princess Kaiulani, who was aptly identified as "a child of heaven." And the all time most popular Hawaiian girl's name, one that has been given to hundreds of local princesses, is, of course, Leilani, or "heavenly *lei.*" Go ahead: Close your eyes, sing the lyrics of "Sweet Leilani, heavenly flower," and see if visions of Paradise don't do a beautiful *hula* through your mind and carry you "Beyond the Reef."

Facing page: A *numbah one* **surfer checks out the view** *and* **surf at Waikiki, and what he spots, above, is a friend banking into a "rad" cutback at the Kaiser's surfing break.**

Above: At Makaha Beach on Oahu's west shore, a well-tanned local pushes his boogie board through a gnarly backwash wave.

In the end, all these individual visions of Paradise float like fluffy clouds in the mind of every Paradise-seeker — whether he or she wants them to or not. Nearly everybody who calls this place home — or merely visits Hawaii — eventually finds something that lends at least temporary credence to that sometimes overly used term. She may be the beautiful *hapa* maiden who graces the cover of this book, or perhaps a white rainbow that appears mysteriously over Mauna Kea on a misty full moon night. It may take a while to weaken your will to resist, but like a little emerald flash that follows sunset, a curious warm feeling will hit you and make that otherworldly word — *Paradise* — come tumbling out.

In his *A Dream of Islands,* sometime Honolulu resident Daws recounts how different voyagers, authors, artists and outright scammers have for more than 200 years chased about Polynesia, "the most seductive place on earth," looking for "physically beautiful brown-skinned men and women [who] move through a living dream of great erotic power." What such people were looking for, and are still looking for, he writes, is not so much an idyllic place on the map, but "a state of mind — a dream of islands."

Hedonistic motives may differ these days, but that langourous lure is alive and well in Hawaii, whether one wants to admit it, or indeed even cares about such romantic concepts. There's something about flying into this place, packing away all your stuffy, cold weather clothes, and changing into a loose *aloha* shirt and rubber slippers, that almost immediately makes this state-of-mind a tangible and emotional reality. Add the fragrance and symbolism of a flower *lei*, and a tropical breeze across your cheeks, and even the most jaded cynic will fall into a state of suspended disbelief.

David Butwin, a former *Honolulu Advertiser* reporter who left Hawaii years ago to become the travel editor of *Saturday Review* magazine, recalled recently how he returned to Hawaii after a long absence and asked himself: "Has the magic vanished?" After observing recent social and economic problems that had made life here more "modern" and "difficult," he concluded that "even the maligned [island of] Oahu can be irresistible at times.

"I am thinking," Butwin wrote, "of those winter mornings when the mynahs strut on the dewy Kapiolani Park lawn, a pair of snowy white doves take flight for Diamond Head, and early bird surfers ride in toward Waikiki on perfect curlers; afternoons when shadows fill the dark green clefts of the Koolau Mountains; early evenings as the sampans and dinner catamarans sail into an orange-sherbet sunset . . ."

Above: If you're in Hawaii during the winter, be sure to catch the wave action at Oahu's infamous Banzai Pipeline surf spot. This particular gallery of wave watchers looks on in awe as a transluscent Pipeline curl begins to do its thing.

Nearly a hundred years earlier, another traveling writer, Robert Louis Stevenson, wrote scathingly about how "in vile Honolulu there are too many cesspools and beastly *haoles.*" In a more meditative moment, however, he gushed about Waikiki's "lovely scenery, quiet, pure air, clear sea water, good food, and heavenly sunsets hung out over the Pacific and the distant hills of Waianae." Again, Paradise lost, then found.

Perhaps because she is so comfortably intimidating, and not as *urbane* as other *civilized* places, visiting cynics take a particular pleasure in kicking Hawaii around like a great grass-skirted dog. The *New Yorker* magazine, for example, has regularly derided Hawaii as "A Sugar-Coated Fortress" and as the "Isles of Disenchantment," and a visiting British journalist recently commented—following a two week research tour—that "yes, Hawaii's a nice place—if you're a pineapple."

Ah, but *no huhu,* brah. Don't be upset. Forget all that pooh-poohing and sniping, and go easy. Hang loose, Hawaiian-style. Stretch out on the beach with all the other cha-lang-a-lang types and sing about wanting to go back to "my little grass shack in Kealakekua, Haw-vahhh-eeee." Or do the Slack Key Samba, like they used to do 'em back in the Thirties.

"I remember the first time I drove through Waikiki," says a recent immigrant from South Carolina. "I could

Above: Master Pipeline rider Gerry Lopez tucks into a tasty blue-green tube during a recent winter surfing contest on Oahu.
Right top: Former world surfing champion Margo Oberg poses with her soon to be surfing son and a quiver of her favorite surfboards in front of her home near Poipu, Kauai.
Right bottom: Honolulu designer Daphne Chu blends in with the surfy symbolism on a radio station KIKI mobile broadcast van.

Bill Barnfield
Bill Barnfield
Bill Barnfield
Bill Barnfield

KIKI

Hawaii has hundreds of the world's finest beaches, many of them in remote and rarely-visited places. At left and at top right are two of Kauai's most "secret" beaches, and at left, a father helps his daughter build sand castles at Puako Bay on the Big Island's peaceful Kohala Coast.

116

actually smell the suntan lotion on people two blocks away from the beach. It was mid-day, the wind was blowin' onshore, it was kind of hot, and a strong chocolate-coconut fragrance was in the air. And when I finally got to the beach, it looked to me like old pictures of Coney Island. You had to step over people's bodies to get to the water. But, oh boy, some of those bodies!"

One could do worse on a sunny weekend than have to subject oneself to tip-toeing over semi-nude bodies, but what that southerner's comments illustrate is that, above all, whether this is a paradise or not, Hawaii is first and foremost a very *sensual* place—or at least a place where people feel guilty if the don't get down to as little clothes as possible and regularly *get close to nature*.

Duke Kahanamoku, the late and great former Olympic swimming champion and the acknowledged "father" of modern surfing, used to say to friends that Hawaii's air and water promote a more than usual sexual appetite. "When the sun shines on their stomachs for a long time," he said, rubbing the area of his solar plexus, "the *wahines* really start thinking about men. And the more sun they get," he would wink, "the mo bettah they get."

Perhaps it is such solar sensuality that gave birth to the bikini, that splendid little two-piece garment that allows the Hawaiian sun to intimidate a lady's solar plexus to da max. In case you didn't know it, brah, it was in Hawaii that the bikini made its first big and stylish debut. This took place at a late 1950s fashion show luncheon held at Waikiki's old and usually staid Halekulani Hotel. For the first time in anybody's memory, a group of well-tanned local ladies paraded around in skimpy two piece bathing wear, and the gathered public's enthusiastic (and shocked) response set journalists' typewriters ablaze with chauvinistic stories that reached the world's fashion centers. It was a *manini* (small) event by tolerant standards, but that premier bikini-showing generated big-eyed headlines around the world. One commentator on the scene nicknamed this provocative beach garment a "bikini," because it had the same effect on viewers as atomic bomb blasts that were held during the Forties on Bikini Island in the northern Pacific's Marshall Islands. The world's press picked up on this ooh-phemism, and the word was soon adopted as part of America's fashion vernacular. Even Webster's Dictionary now notes that the term was adopted "for the comparison of the effects wrought by a scantily clad woman to the effects of an atomic bomb." Today, of course, such Hawaii-born beachwear is the pleasant rule throughout Polynesia — and the world.

But enough of such sexuality. Let us instead "get physical" and remember that there is more to Hawai-

Above: A pair of genteel locals enjoy the sunshine and view from their suburban home atop Honolulu's Waialae Iki Ridge.
Right: An aquamarine islet sits like a little jewel in waters near Laie on Oahu's surf-pounded North Shore.

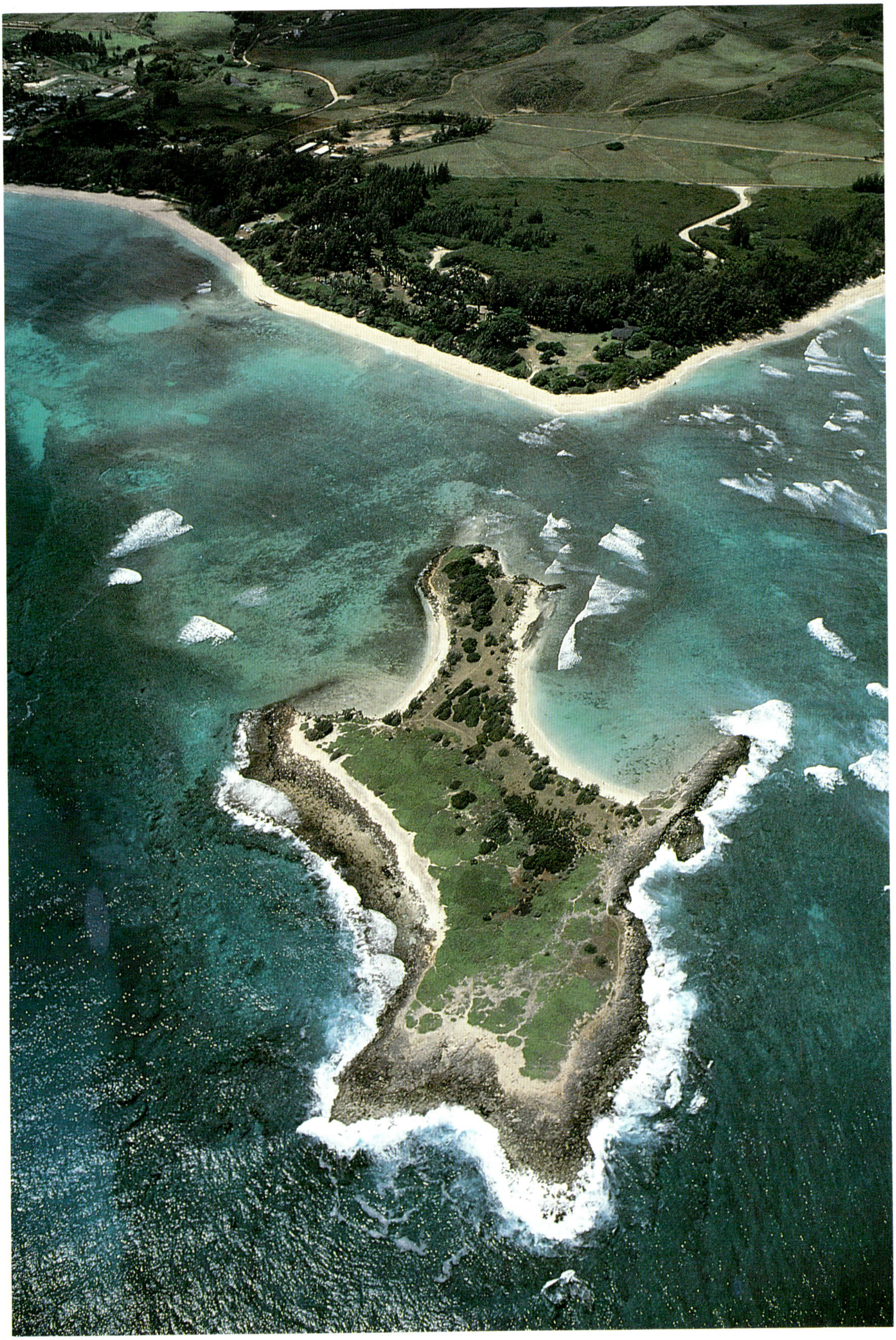

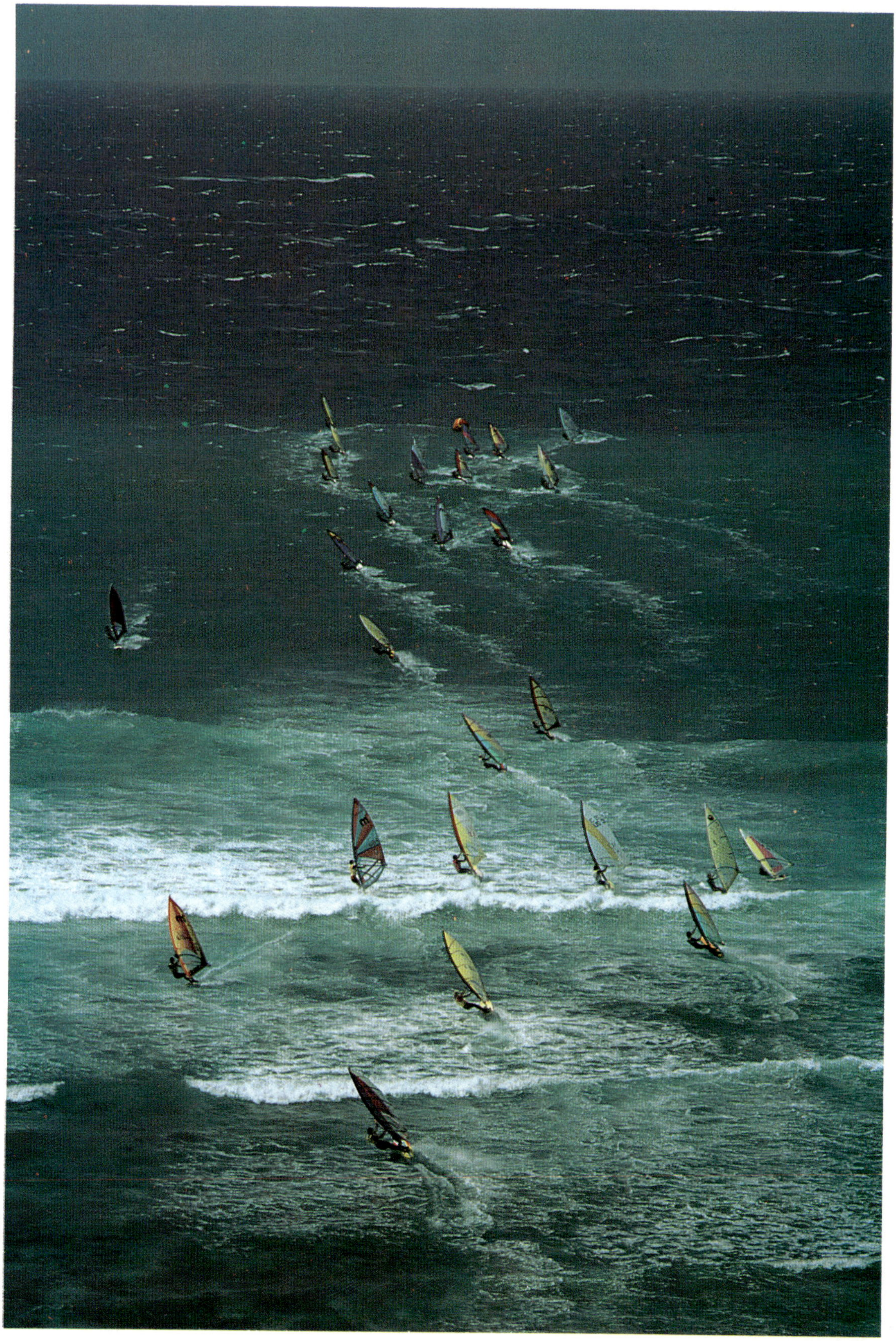

ian sensuality than *hula* girls, loose-fitting *aloha* shirts and *muumuus,* and well-turned women walking up and down the sands of fashion.

Ask a surfer about Hawaii, and he'll spend hours describing the nuance and sheer power of "the most perfect waves in the world." He'll tell you all about how that sport was born here, and how ancient Hawaiians used to play on nature's waves like dolphins lost in distant and sparkling seas. Even windsurfing, that new watersport that is sweeping the world, was born here, and continues to flourish here in a "state of the art" style.

As important as the actual practicing of sports such as surfing and windsurfing, however, is the influence that these athletic pursuits have had on the rest of the world. In recent years, surfers and windsurfers have carried their sports and lifestyles far away from Hawaii, and in the process have spawned a billion dollars a year fashion industry that has literally changed the "look" of sportswear cool throughout the wet (and dry) world. And if you don't believe it, brah, check out the Hawaiian styles now being worn in the world's most hip resorts. Da Hawaiian look, or *surf chic* if you will, is what's happening and in fashion.

This "Made in Paradise" business can, and often does, take the form of well-intentioned feelings packed in a commercial and heavy syrup, but it can also be ex-

When it comes to that new international water-sport called "windsurfing," Hawaii is da best place to strut your "slash and burn" stuff. Facing page: A fleet of late afternoon board sailors tack and come about off Diamond Head, and above left and right, two of their number fly high and mostly dry.

plained and experienced in very ingenuous ways. Consider, for example, the first time that a Hawaiian friend smiles broadly and affectionately bids you *aloha*. He could be a jive Hawaiian who's simply telling you what you want to hear, but more often than not he's using a beautiful word which in its purest form is addressing your spirit, or the breath of life that resides within you.

Don Chapman, who writes a daily morning "talk over the fence" column for *The Honolulu Advertiser*, recalled in a recent interview how he was poignantly introduced to "paradise" and the so-called "aloha spirit."

"It was my first week in Hawaii, about five years ago," he said, "and I was at the Halekulani Hotel having drinks and enjoying an evening of Hawaiian music. During the course of the evening, I was introduced to the late *hula* master Auntie Maiki Aiu Lake. I told her I was new in town and would be writing a daily column for *The Advertiser*. When I told her I was a little worried about my new job, being a recently-arrived Coast *haole* with little knowledge about Hawaii, she took me aside and said: 'Don't worry. Just go outside, take off your shoes, walk barefoot in the sand, feel the surf between your toes, hear the rustling of the palm trees, then look up at the mountains, the stars and the moon. See and feel these things, and if you love these things, you'll also love Hawaii.'"

**Above: Local waterman Robbie Naish, a Kailuan widely regarded to be windsurfing's biggest individual "star," flashes a "shaka" sign for our cameraman in waters off Diamond Head.
Right: Got a hot dog who wants to cool off? Take him windsurfing. This particular mutt is enjoying a cruise off Oahu's Lanikai Beach.**

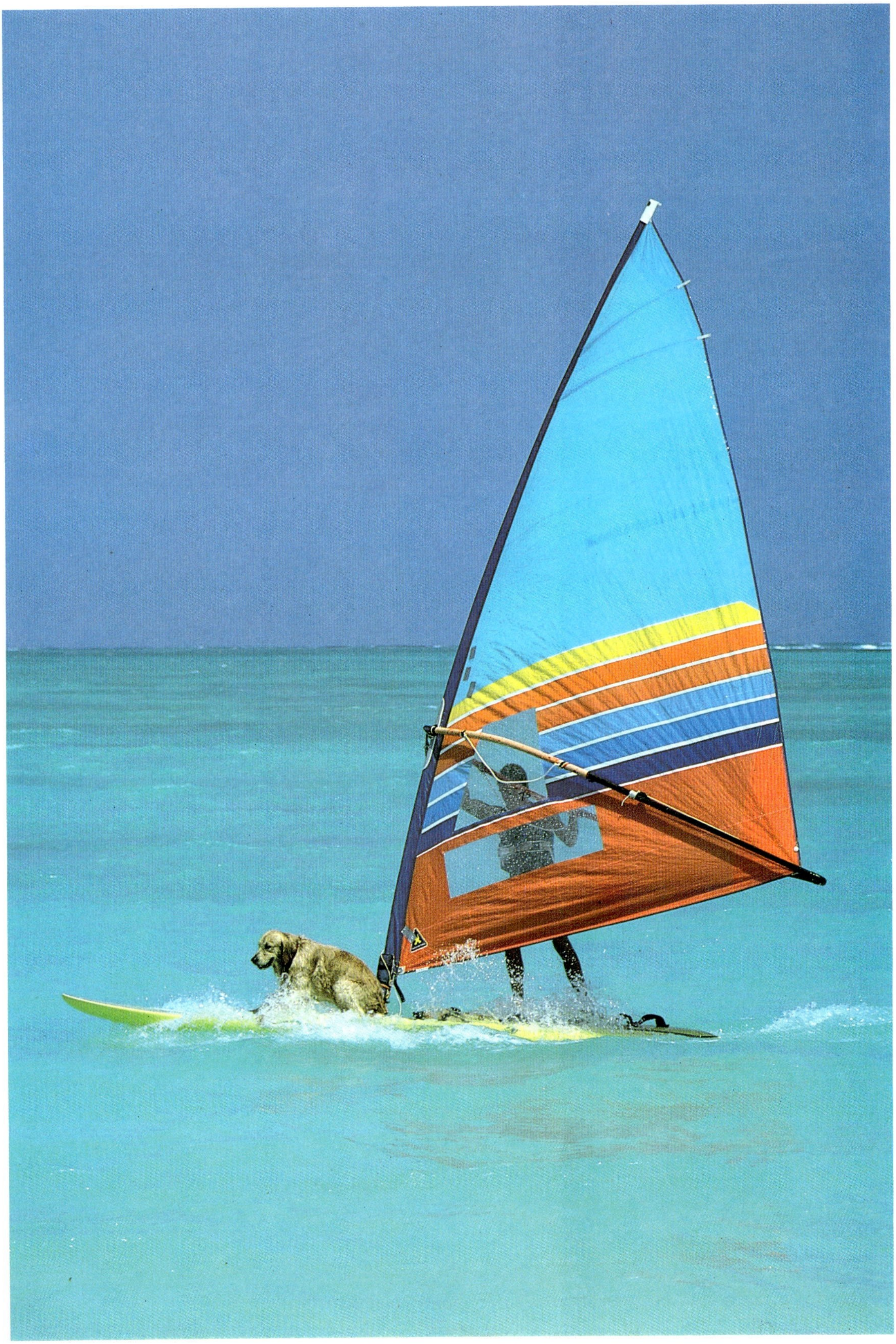

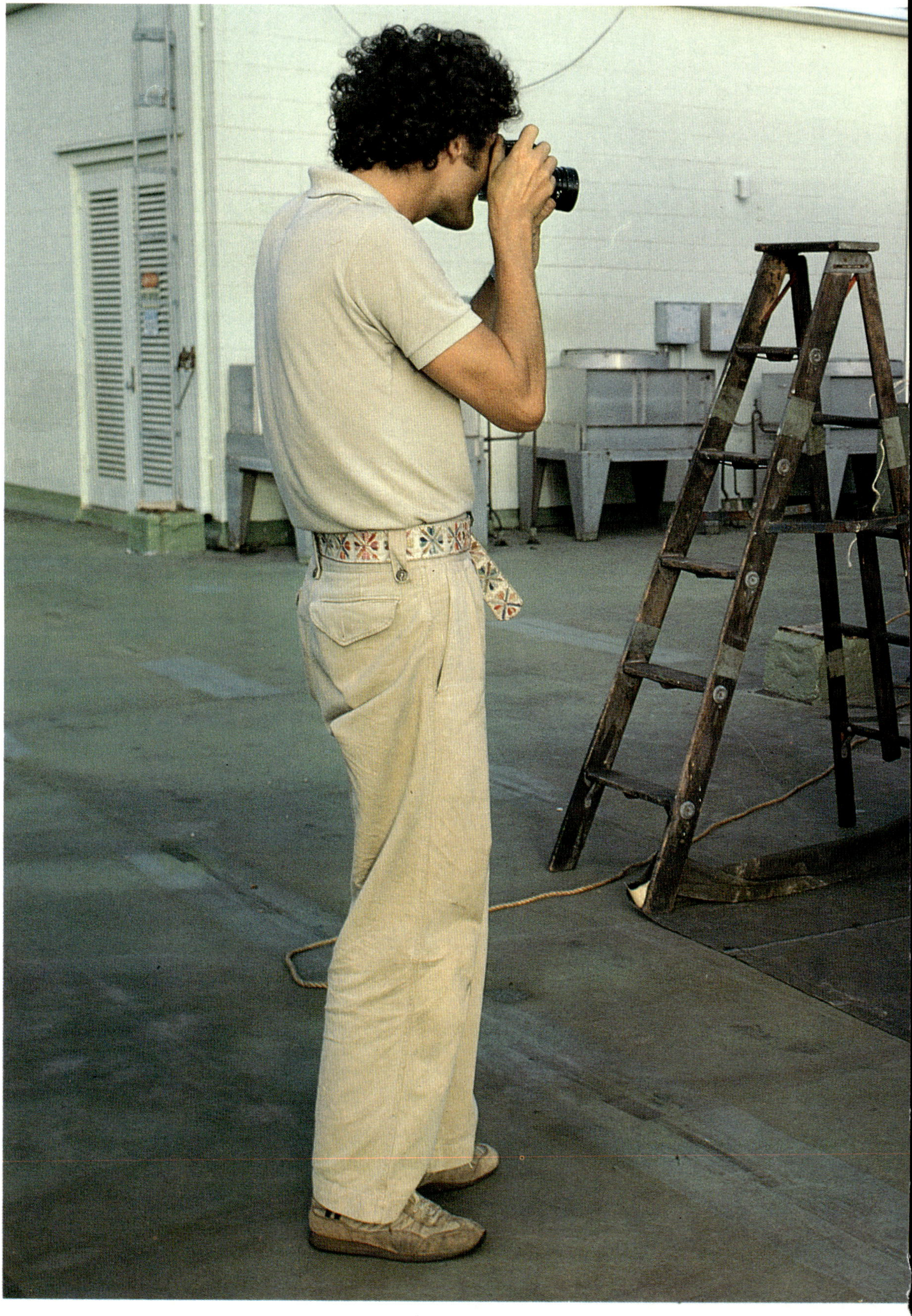

Left: A visiting European photographer frames the *hula* maiden of his dreams, while yet other *hula* girls, above, perform on the animated cover of a Waikiki memorabilia pad.

Above: A Volcano-area dancer honors the fire goddess Pele during a recent *hula* performance above Kilauea Crater, the Big Island. Right: Lucky visitors to the Hawaii Volcanoes National Park marvel at and pose before a 1982 lava flow that closed off the Volcano area's Chain of Craters road.

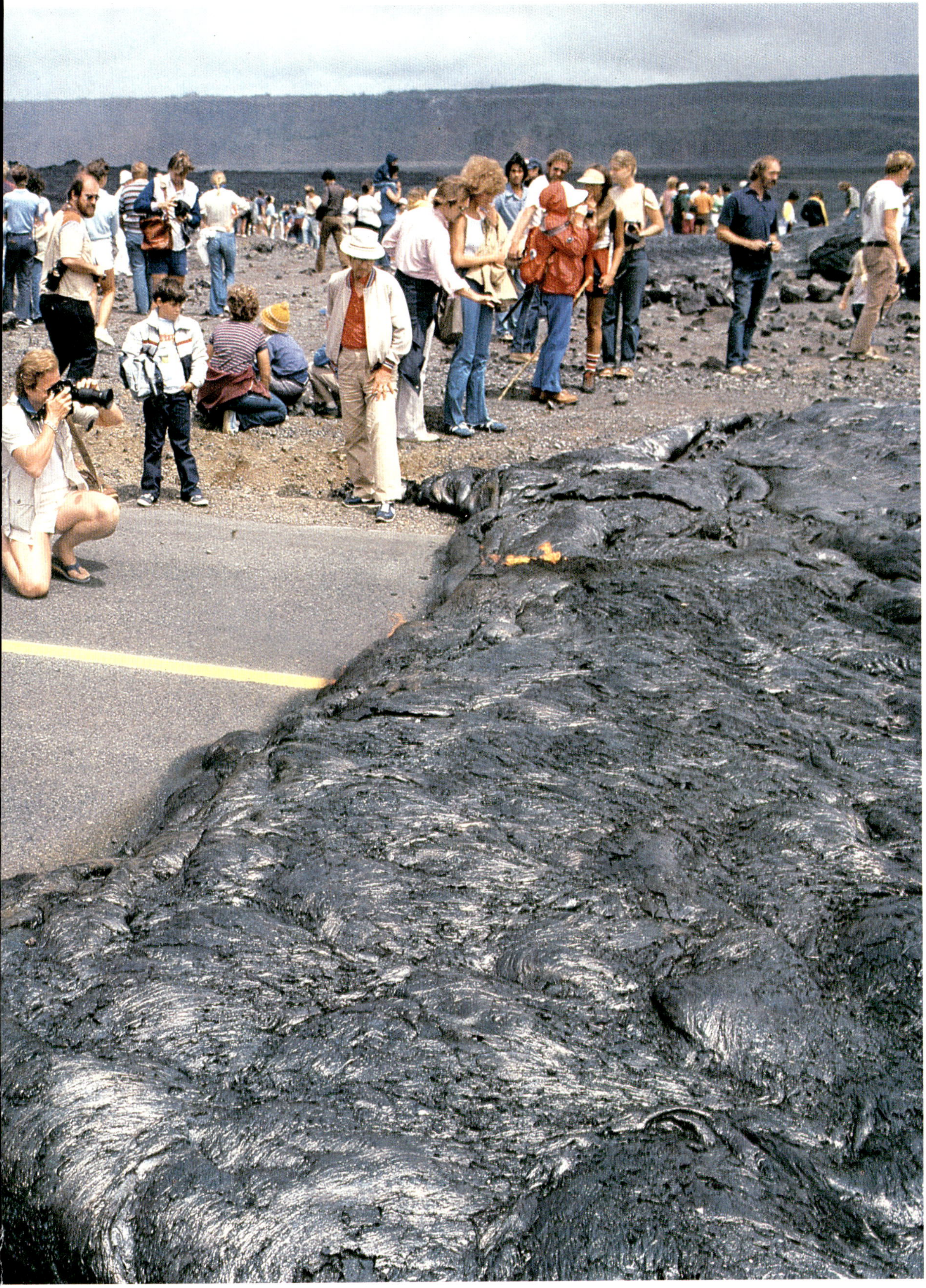

Above: A winsome tour guide poses and preens for a passing visitor's camera. Right: *Kialoa,* a world class ocean-racing yacht warms up for Hawaii's popular round-the-state sailing regatta in waters off beautiful Waikiki-by-the-sea.

128

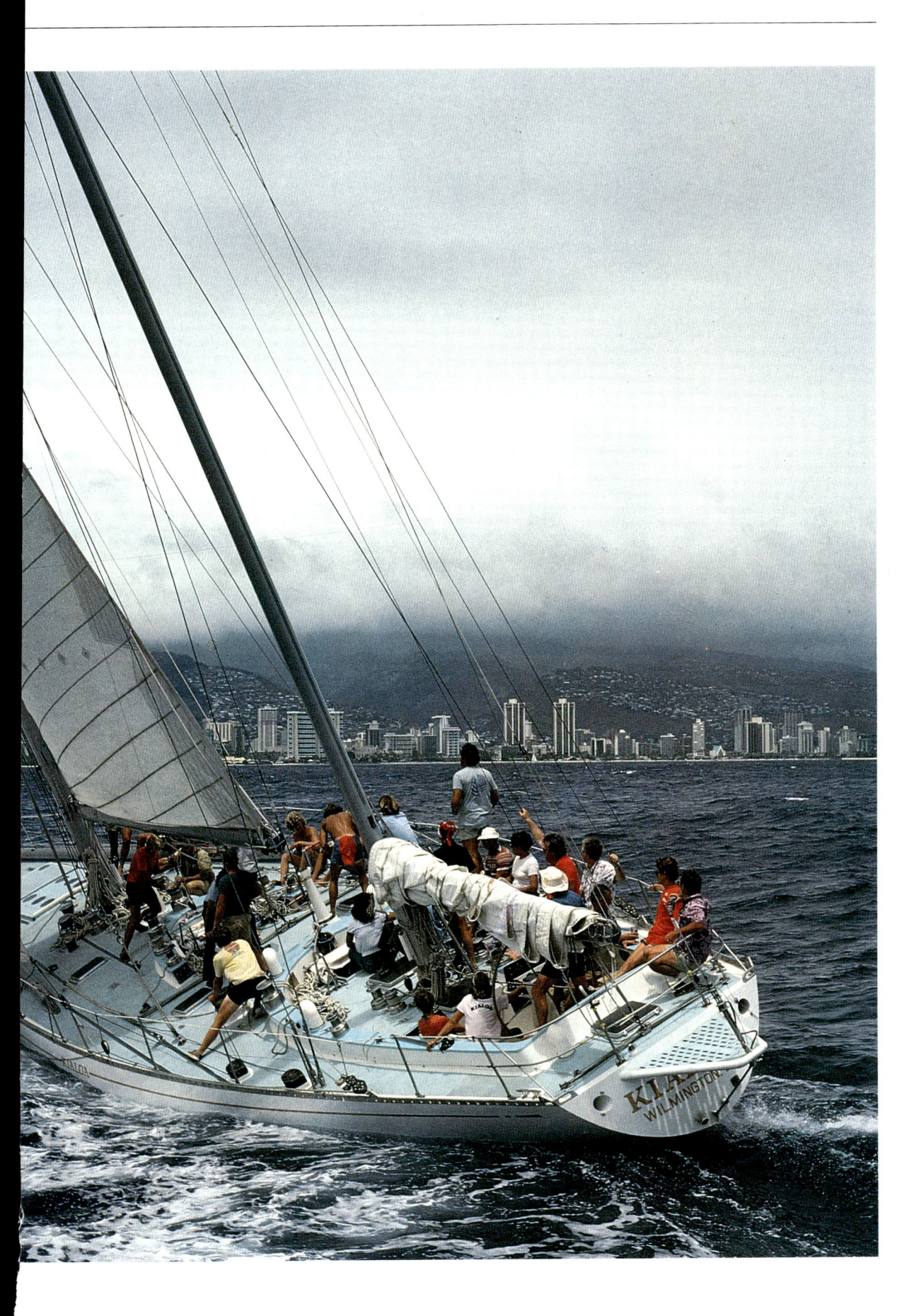
WILMINGTON

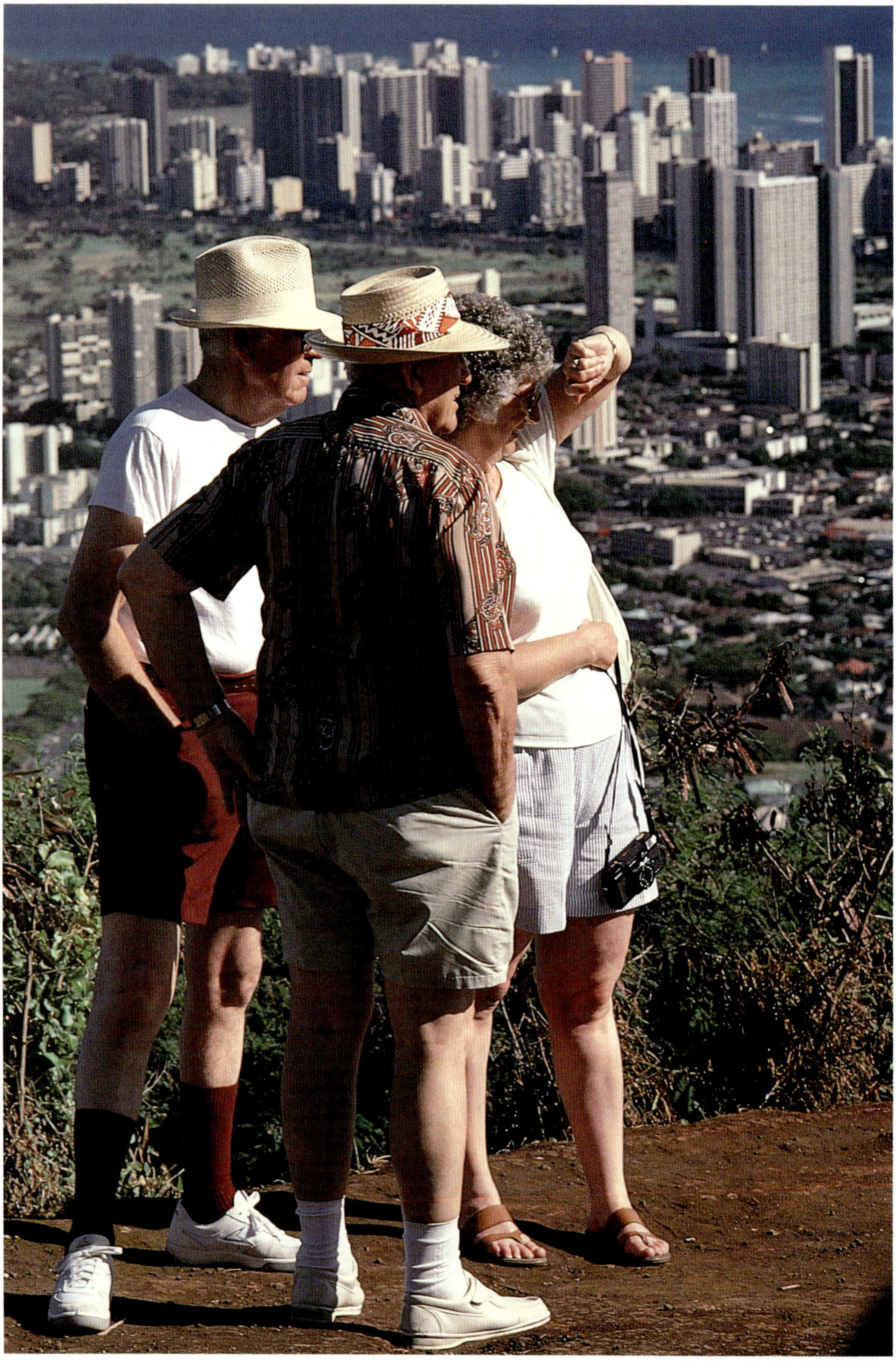

*Tourists here, tourists there
Tourists sitting 'round everywhere,
In short-shorts and* muumuus *too,
Trying to do like the Hawaiians do.*

—*Refrain from an old
Waikiki beachboy song.*

The original and probably still the best "guidebook" impressions ever written about Hawaii were those penned by the British Captain James Cook and his Lieutenant James King. Their Hawaii accounts, published in the British Admiralty's three volumes about *A Voyage to the Pacific Ocean, 1776–1780,* were the first of hundreds of Hawaii-related publications to report in romantic detail what this land of *hula* maidens, surfers, *kalua* pig and sticky *poi* is all about. Like all good and evocative guidebooks, the Cook-King volumes (fabulously illustrated by the artist to the expedition, John Webber) set thousands of faraway minds abuzz with visions of a new Paradise Found.

During the last two decades of the 18th Century and the early part of the 19th Century, dozens of sailing ships from other nations began calling on Cook's fabled Sandwich Isles, and the many stories and "images" written, sketched and painted by their shipboard authors and artists became all the rage in America, England and on The Continent. Armchair travelers oohed and ahed, and Hawaii—or *Owyhee* as it was then spelled—quickly became a *must* stop on every Pacific voyager's itinerary. Eminent explorers with names like Kotzebue, La Perouse and Vancouver sailed here, soaked up local culture and sunshine, and left to once again *spread the word* about a "Paradise of the Pacific" that *should not be missed.*

Today, perhaps a billion words, brush strokes and camera clicks later, tourism, or "the visitor industry" if you will, continues to grow like a wild, rainbow-colored virus in a warm petri dish. The going was gracious and slow as a steamship during pre-aviation days, but as recently as 1946, the year after World War II ended, some 15,000 people crossed the Pacific and holidayed in Hawaii. That's not too many *maitai*-drinkers, but that figure quadrupled to 60,000 a year by 1966, and then surged like a human tidal wave to 3.2 million in 1976. "How you figgah?" asked local tour guides, but this annual human wave grew even bigger and by 1983 some 4.3 million visitors a year were jetting and sailing into Alohaland!

Facing page: "Look mom, no smog!" A trio of Bermuda-shorted visitors admires the sweeping view of Oahu from a park atop Honolulu's cool Mount Tantalus. That's high rising Waikiki beyond.
Above: A snow white bride and groom from Osaka pose for a post-wedding portrait that is part and parcel of their carefully packaged Hawaiian wedding and honeymoon tour. Hawaii is one of Japan's most-favored overseas vacation—and marital—destination.

Nobody's quite sure how long this accelerated growth will continue, but Honolulu economists predict that tourism will boom on and be this state's major source of income at least through the rest of this century. "After more than two centuries of entertaining foreign guests and 25 years as America's 50th state," reported a recent story in the *Honolulu Star-Bulletin,* "Hawaii is confident that it can continue to lure visitors from both East and West for fun and sun in the middle of the Pacific . . . State planners say that by the year 2005, Hawaii's 1.3 million residents can be expected to play host to more than 8 million tourists annually."

Did they say 8 million visitors a year? In little Hawaii by the sea? Within the next 20 years? Yup, that's what the experts said, and island minds boggle when considering what that means in terms of *muumuus* to be worn, tropical drinks to be drunk and *kalua* pigs to be slaughtered for the thousands of *luaus* that will be held here during the next two decades. I mean, really brah, how many *ukulele* tinkling baritones and lithe Tahitian belly dancers will we need to entertain 8 million Paradise-seekers a year? And who's going to pick and string all those flower *leis*? And kiss all those just arrived cheeks? And mix all those *maitais*?

Whoever does what to whom, or for whom, you can bet that dreams will continue to come true in "Blue

While one Tahitian doll strums a tiny *ukulele,* dozens of others do the *tamure,* a distant cousin of the Hawaiian *hula.* Such colorful gee-gaws dominate shelf space in shopping arcades and roadside stalls throughout Waikiki-by-the-sea.

Sharkskin drums thunder, hips begin swaying, and a recent VIP visitor sips fresh pineapple juice. This particular tourist, at left, is Zhao Ziyang, Premier of the State Council of the People's Republic of China. Zhao visited Hawaii in 1984.

Hawaii." Those millions of visitors will hop out of bigger and shinier airplanes, buses and taxis, outfit themselves in even more garish Polynesian attire, plop into warm Hawaiian waters, and—before flying back to Keokuk and Osaka—have the sunshiney, Hawaiian times of their lives.

Their opening scenario, with a Honolulu dateline, will probably remain something like this typical letter from faraway and romantic Hawaii:

Dear Mom,

I know you've probably been worrying about me, wondering where I am and all, but I had to wait a few days, convince myself that I really am here, and then let you know that I impulsively got on an airplane, left New York in a snowstorm, and at this very moment I'm sitting on a sunny lanai, *enjoying Kona coffee, guava nectar and Puna papaya — and wondering why I didn't come here sooner. I didn't mean to rush off without calling, but I was sitting in my cold Soho loft last week when the urge hit and I had to leave. The Hawaiian Open golf tournament was being broadcast live from Honolulu, and there was something about the clear blue skies, little flower-covered bikinis and sunburnt faces on the TV screen that made me run down to a travel agency, buy a special package tour*

Above: A pair of Paradise Cruise guides smile and pause for a sun-splashed breather before cruising on with a busload of happy tourists. Left: Da boys and one local girl compare tans on the beach at Waikiki.

"Hawaiian wear" is now all the rage in other parts of the world, but this local "look" has been *de rigueur* here for some four decades.

ticket, and say ah-low-huh *to the Big Apple. The next morning I strapped myself into a jumbo jet at Kennedy Airport, and – bam! – just like magic – I was here.*

As I stepped out of the airplane, the strains of vampy Hawaiian music filled the air, and before I could even get my suitcase off the baggage carousel, a beautiful island girl draped a pink orchid lei *around my neck, kissed me, and then smiled while a nice young man took our picture. (Picture enclosed. I'm the white person in the blue blazer.)*

Anyway, Mom, all of us on this Happy Hawaiian Holidays tour got into a big, air-conditioned bus and rode past a giant pineapple, waving palm trees and pretty Honolulu Harbor to our fancy hotel overlooking Waikiki Beach. I was tired, but the first thing I did was go for a swim in the warm water. I was only on the beach for about an hour, but whoa, you should have seen me that night: I looked like a pink Florida flamingo, and I couldn't lay on my back for the next two days. It was terrible, and I felt awfully conspicuous around all the well-tanned people here, but you ought to see me now in my Tom Selleck-style shirt, Japanese flip-flops and my new bronze body.

I haven't seen McGarrett or Magnum yet, but last night we took in the Don Ho show. He didn't sing very much, but he kissed a lot of ladies that looked just like you, and before I left his big nightclub, I got him to autograph a picture for your celebrity scrapbook. When I asked him to do that, he said "Ain't no big thing, brah," and then he signed the picture "Love to Lucy. From Don." Then he kissed some more ladies who were lined up in front of his organ and told everybody to "Suck 'em up, loosen up." We did, and that's why I slept until noon today. They call my condition "Polynesian Paralysis."

Would like to write more, Mom, but I've got a surfing lesson in an hour—and only *three more days to work on my Hawaiian tan—so I'll just say* ahhh-looww-huhh *again and promise more details later.*

With love from Paradise. Your son, Marvin.

P.S.: Tell Dad he'd get a big kick out of all the Japanese tourists who visit the Arizona Memorial at Pearl Harbor. And tell him that his old wartime hangout, The Hubba-Hubba Bar, is still full of American GIs... and girls!

They're a strange flock of birds, these tourists, and those of us lucky enough to live here are always amazed by their other-worldly antics. They appear to be normal workaday folks from Everytown U.S.A., Japan or Elsewhere, but once they've been deposited into their hotels and had a rummy look at a first Hawaiian sunset, their eyes glaze over and they become like big children

Above: King Birendra Bir Bikram Shah Dev of the Himalayan kingdom of Nepal completes a formal courtesy visit to the *USS Arizona* **Memorial at Pearl Harbor during the course of a recent royal visit.**
Right: An afternoon aerial view of the Arizona Memorial. This stylized memorial, designed by Honolulu architect Alfred Preis, recalls the infamous bombing of Pearl Harbor on December 7, 1941.

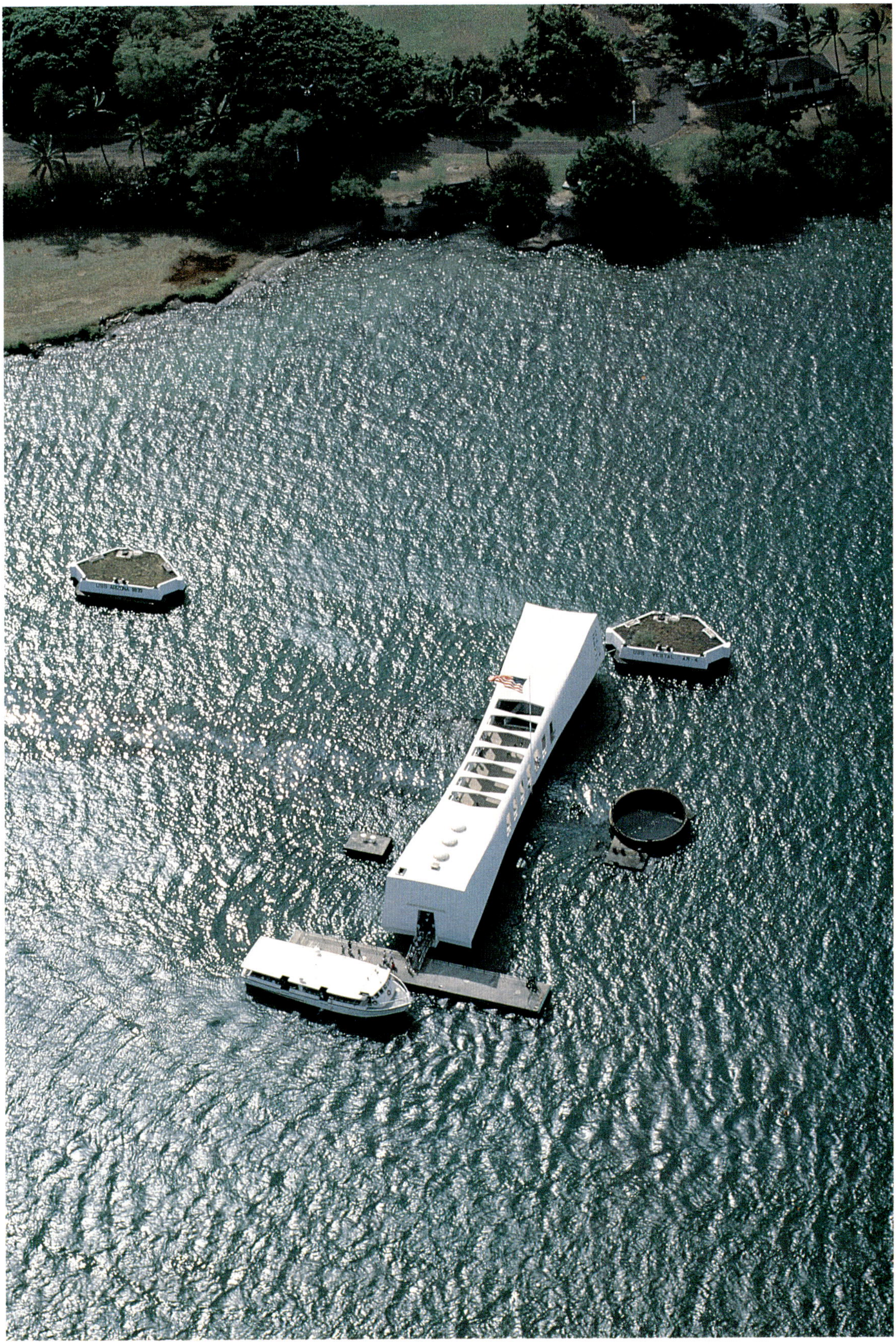

in a giant sandbox. Take a leisurely stroll through Waikiki, "The World's Most Famous Beach," and you'll see them wandering up and down busy Kalakaua Avenue like innocents lost on an air-conditioned and neon-lit desert isle. They smile blissfully as surfer boys (and girls) pedal them here and there in Paradise Pedicabs; they buy coconuts with seascapes painted on them; and they drink potent Chi-Chis, Blue Hawaiis and Tropical Itches underneath flickering Tiki Torches. *"Ah-low-huh"* a tour guide will bellow for the tenth time, and they all smile—Japanese, Americans, all of them—and respond with a long and thunderous *"Ah-low-huh"* that makes banana muffins tremble on a nearby buffet table.

Outside, in the warm tradewinds, they wear T-shirts that proclaim "I Got Lei'd Hawaiian Style" or "Where's The Beach?" and file into Paradise Cruise buses bound for cultural centers, bird parks, sunset booze cruises, *luaus,* Pearl Harbor, *muumuu* factories and dozens of other such visitor attractions. "Hop Aboard The Free Hilo Hattie Bus." "You're Invited To A Free Macadamia Nut Tasting." "Visit Hawaii's Largest Liquidation Center For Name Brand Aloha Shirts and Shortie-Muus." "Relax Island-Style On the Hula Kai Catamaran." "Have Your Picture Taken, Standing On A Surfboard, Surrounded By the Sights and Sounds of Hawaii's Most Awesome Wave." "See Seven Islands In One Day!" The signs and attractions are everywhere, and if a visitor still doesn't know what to do, he or she can pick up free copies of *Spotlight Hawaii, Island News, Guide to Hawaii, On the Go Hawaii, Island Guide, Paradise News, Here in Hawaii, This Week On Oahu,* the *Waikiki Beach Press* or a half dozen other publications that lead him or her to wet T-shirt nights, U.S. Army and Elvis Presley museums or Sunday afternoon bikini contests. "One, two, now one, two, now vamp!" yells the leader of a *hula*-aerobics class, and the scene gets campier with the rise of every palm-framed moon.

"Waikiki. At night when the shadows are falling, I hear your rolling surf calling. Magic across the sea. Waikiki." As the Auntie Mahulani Trio sings those words in a shrill Hawaiian falsetto, an aloha-shirted black dude from Chicago sighs, turns to his wife and says: "Yes, jive mama, here we are, in the world famous Keys. Bee-yoo-tee-ful Wai-key-key." A few minutes later, along Kuhio Avenue's infamous "Red Curb District," another well-turned mama in red spike heels walks up to him, jiggles, and asks, "Wanna date?" but our man in the Keys calls his real mama, says "No thank you, baby," and tips on by.

On yet another street corner, a pair of jaded travelers seeking refuge from smoggy L.A. considers row upon

One of Oahu's most popular longtime attractions is Sea Life Park at Makapuu, and that aquatic marineland's most charming resident is a docile killer whale, far left, left and above, who daily leaps, pirouettes and smiles for visiting audiences.

row of little kiosks crammed to their thatchy rafters full of Polynesian gee-gaws. While licking at *lilikoi* sherbets, they marvel at the kiosks' vast collections of *hula* girl ashtrays, surfing Snoopies, plastic palm trees, crystal pineapples and "surfer wallets" engraved with the words "Hang Loose, Shaka Hawaii!" Yes, Coney Island and/or Tijuana gone troppo. "But did you see that little *hula* girl down by the Ala Wai," says one traveler to another.

"One thing we've learned during the past ten years," says a prosperous Waikiki shopkeeper, "is that very few business people here have lost money underestimating the visiting public's taste. It's those who have tried to appeal to the upper-class or intellectual tastes who have had problems."

Sure, there are also lots of mega-bucks hideaways where "up-market" visitors can lose themselves in little blue cabanas on private crescents of sand, but they are costly exceptions and reminders of Hawaii's *old days* when most visitors arrived on elegant steamships with nannies and accountants in tow and spent entire summers learning how to surf and relax. These days the average budget-proof visitor is here for 6 to 10 days, and he or she is usually part of a finely-tuned package tour.

Local folks, however, *relate* to such lucrative concepts, smile pleasant and tolerant smiles, and simply regard places like Waikiki, Lahaina, Kona and other

Above: Three visitors admire the texture of a cloth mural on view in the lobby of the posh Mauna Lani Bay resort hotel on the Big Island's Kohala Coast, while in other nearby Kohala places we enjoy aerial views of the Mauna Lani's isolated beach, above right, and the sprawling Pu'ukohola Heiau. This *heiau* was built by the famous Hawaiian king, Kamehameha the Great, in honor of his fearsome war God named Kuka'ilimoku.

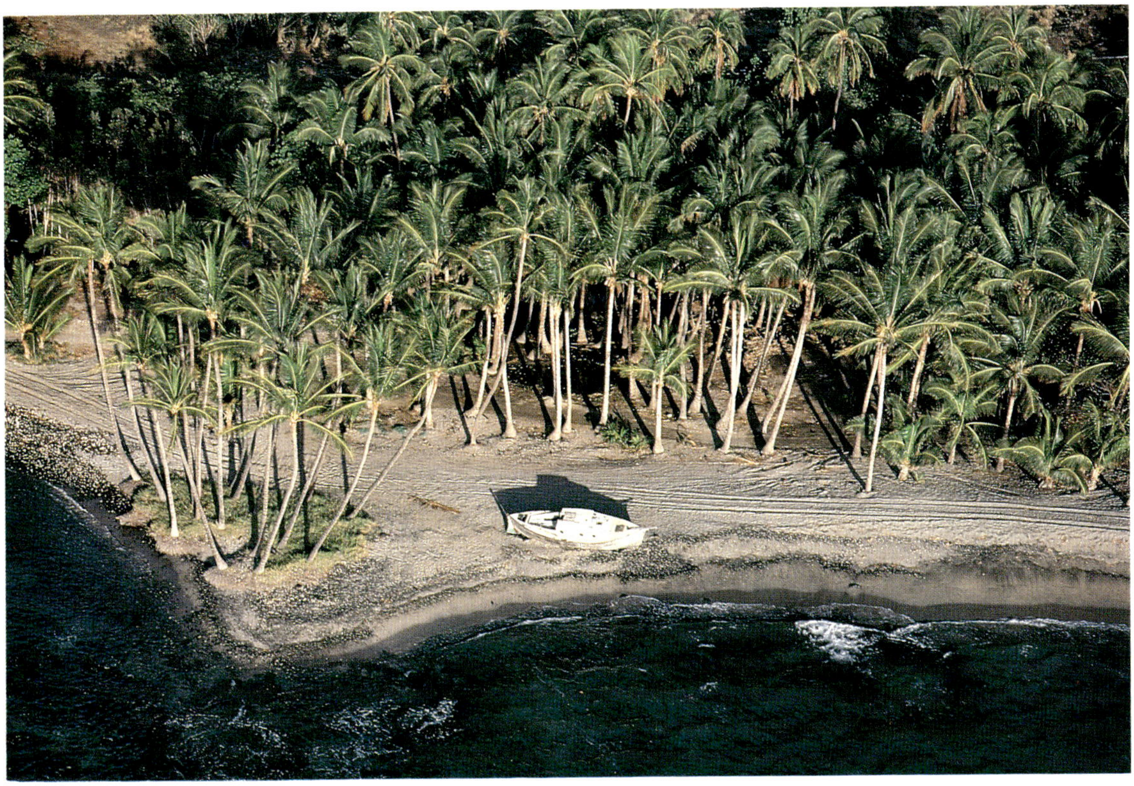

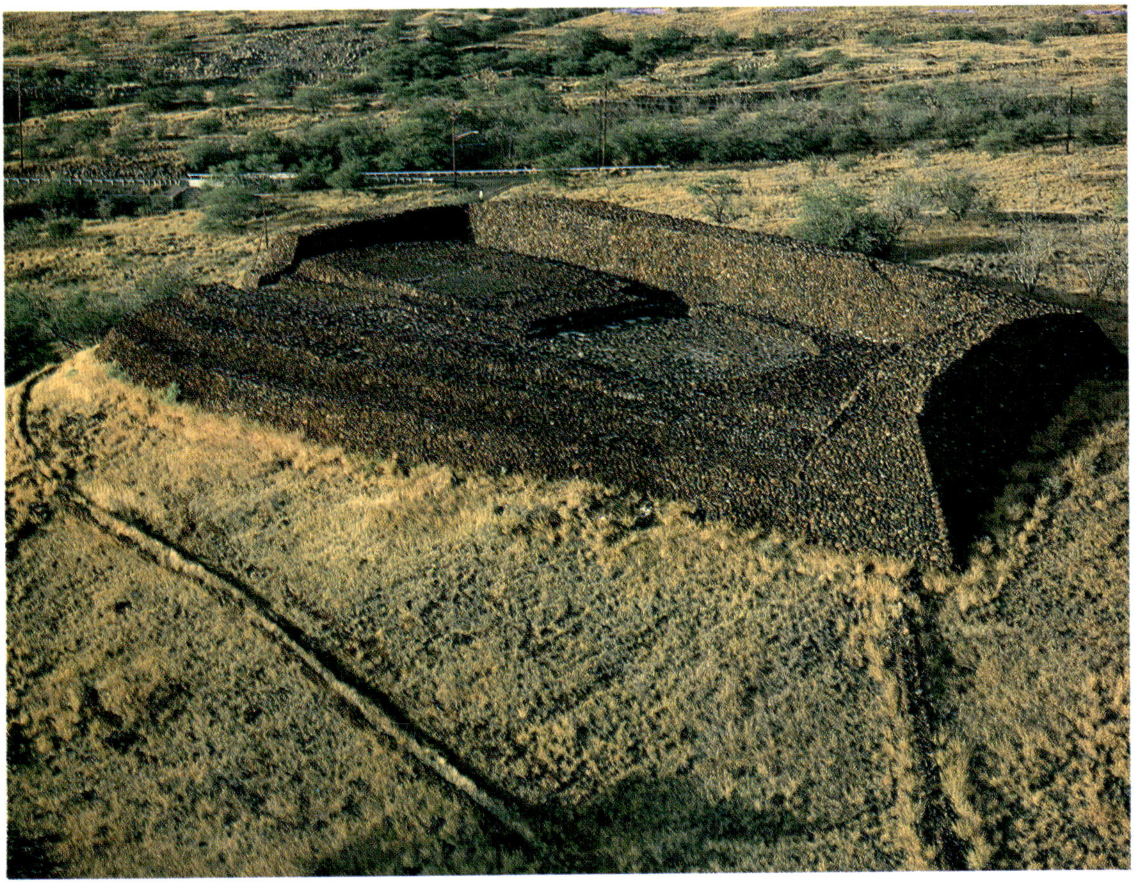

Hawaiian resort areas as curious free-fire zones where *anything goes* and lots of strange but apparently happy people spend lots of money supporting our economy. "I mean, really, nobody who lives here goes into Waikiki during the week," a *kamaaina* (long time) resident sniffs. That matron is engaging in a bit of local girl snobbery, but she's not far from the truth. Unless a landed Honoluluan is one of those rare 23,000 or so people who actually live in Waikiki, or if he or she makes his or her living serving the visitor industry, he or she spends precious little time in these transient enclaves. And unless you live next door to a so-called tourist attraction, you will rarely ever encounter or be disturbed by a tourist — unless you can see one through the dark tinted or silver mirrored windows of the many fast-moving tour buses that circle and criss-cross the islands every day.

Yes, we aloof islanders like to poke fun at these big-eyed visitors passing through our suburbs and natural wonders, but deep down we understand — though guardedly and protectively — why people insist on coming here in ever-increasing numbers. We understand indeed, but like all people who have beautiful but wide open secrets, we ask just one thing: Please don't tell anybody else about this special place called Hawaii. They might want to live here too.

Above: An interisland cruise ship cum "loveboat" frames a fine sunset off Waikiki, and right, just down from Waikiki, yet another trademark Hawaiian sunset backlights Oahu's Diamond Head lighthouse.

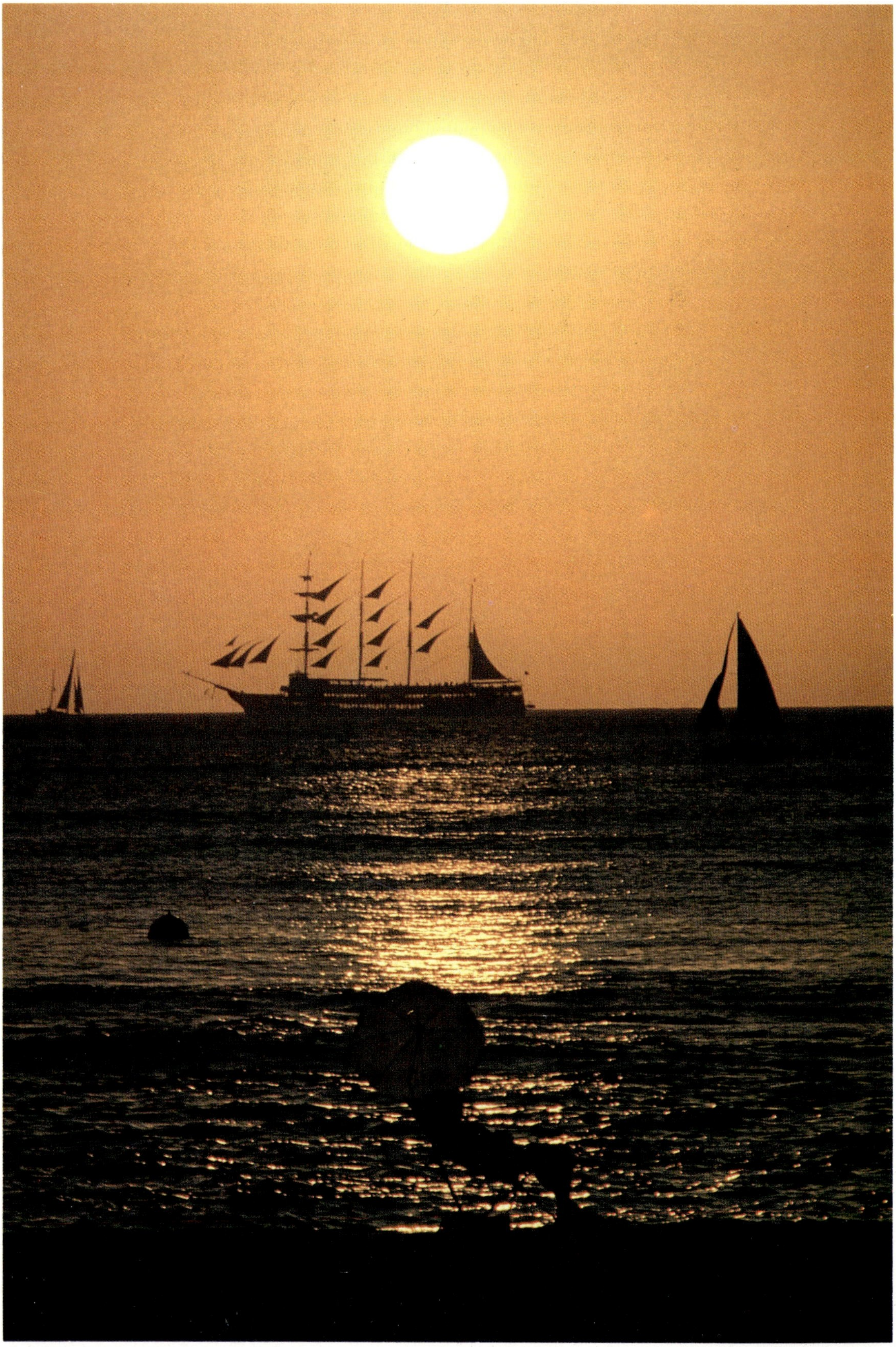